NAPOLEON HILL'S GOLDEN RULES

NAPOLEON HILL

WILEY

John Wiley & Sons, Inc.

Published by John Wiley & Sons, Inc., Hoboken, New Jersey.
Published simultaneously in Canada.

For general information on our other products and services or for technical support, please contact our Customer Care Department within the United States at (800) 762-2974, outside the United States at (317) 572-3993 or fax (317) 572-4002.

Wiley also publishes its books in a variety of electronic formats. Some content that appears in print may not be available in electronic books. For more information about Wiley products, visit our web site at www.wiley.com.

Library of Congress Cataloging-in-Publication Data:

Hill, Napoleon, 1883–1970.
  Napoleon Hill's golden rules: the lost writings / Napoleon Hill.
      p.   cm.
  Includes bibliographical references and index.
  ISBN 978-0-470-41156-8 (pbk.)
  1. Success in business. 2. Positive psychology. I. Title. II. Title: Golden rules.
  HF5386.H562 2009
  650.1–dc22   2008038666

Printed in the United States of America

10 9 8 7 6

MORALITY CANNOT BE FAIRLY
NOR ACCURATELY ACCESSED BY
REFERRING TO HOW OTHERS SEE
YOU!!

CONTENTS

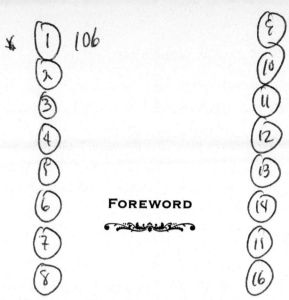

FOREWORD

*P*erhaps you are like millions the world over who have read Napoleon Hill's writings and have profited from them. Whether you are a follower of Hill's teaching or this is your first encounter with his writing, you will benefit from these lessons on human potential.

The sources of the book you have in your hands are magazines Hill published over eighty years ago. *Hill's Golden Rule Magazine* and *Hill's Magazine* were published for several years before his first book appeared. Hill's lessons are a series of writings on human potential.

The remote mountains of Wise County, Virginia, where Hill was born in 1883, did not provide a lot of opportunities for a boy being raised in poverty. Hill's mother died when he was ten years old, and his father married again a year later. Napoleon's new stepmother was to be a blessing to the young boy. Martha was a young widow who was educated, the daughter of a doctor; she took a liking to her highly energized stepson, who was often involved in mischievous deeds. The newest member of the Hill household was a source of encouragement that lasted a lifetime. Later in life, Hill credited his stepmother in a manner similar to the way Abraham Lincoln, the sixteenth President of the United States, credited his, when he once remarked that "whatever I am or ever aspire to be I owe to that dear woman." By the age of thirteen, with the help of his stepmother, he had traded a pistol for a typewriter. A series of articles would encourage his pursuit of a profession in writing.

After two years of high school, Hill enrolled in a business school, and upon completion sought a job with Rufus Ayres, who had been Attorney General of the State of Virginia, an officer in the Confederacy, and at one time a candidate for the United States Senate. General Ayres was into banking, lumber, and coal mining, and Hill thought of him as the richest man in the mountains. Suddenly attracted to the law profession, however, Hill convinced his brother Vivian to apply with him to Georgetown Law School; Napoleon would work as a writer and pay both of their ways. Both enrolled at Georgetown Law School, and Vivian graduated but Napoleon was detoured, obtaining a job with *Bob Taylor's Magazine*, which was owned by Robert Taylor, a United States Senator from Tennessee. Hill's assignments were success stories, including a story on the growth of Mobile, Alabama, as a seaport. When he was sent to interview Andrew Carnegie at his 45-room mansion, what was scheduled to be a short interview lasted three days. Carnegie challenged him to interview the successful and develop a philosophy of success, which Hill would then teach to others. Hill's life was changed drastically, and his lifelong adventure was to interview successful people in his study of why some were successful and so many others were not.

Carnegie's introduction put the young Hill in contact with Henry Ford, Thomas Edison, George Eastman, John D. Rockefeller, and other noted people of the time. Hill's study of the success principles took twenty years with over five hundred interviews before he wrote his first book.

Hill lived to be 87 years old and during his lifetime developed the philosophy of success principles that are as relevant today as when he studied and recorded his findings in his books. Hill's first title was actually an eight-volume set called *The Law of Success*, published in 1928. He began to receive royalties of $2,000 to $3,000 per month, such a huge sum that he purchased a Rolls-Royce for a visit up Guest River in the mountains of Wise County, Virginia, where he had spent his childhood.

Hill wrote a small book called *The Magic Ladder to Success*, and while it appeared to be a condensed version of *The Law of Success*, it added a section called "Forty Unique Ideas" for making money. Among Hill's ideas were automatic gas filling stations at which motorists could serve themselves either day or night, keyless locks to prevent theft, and fountain drinks made of vegetables served fresh without preservatives. Remember, this was in 1930; the list demonstrates what a visionary Hill was.

Further evidence that Hill was a visionary is found in the fact that so much of the self-help material written today is simply a version of what Hill studied and wrote about over 80 years ago.

Today a number of books have been written about the law of attraction as if it is some newly discovered principle that will ensure success. Hill wrote about this "new" principle in the March 1919 issue of *Hill's Golden Rule Magazine*, which is included in Lesson #4: The Law of Retaliation.

Today there are stacks and stacks of books that reference one or more of Hill's works, and he is no doubt quoted more than any other motivational writer or speaker who ever lived. These quotes are sometimes used verbatim and at other times with slight changes.

In 1937, Hill wrote his most famous book, *Think and Grow Rich*, which sold out three times the year it was published at $2.50 a copy in the middle of the Great Depression, and that was without mass advertising that exists today. *Think and Grow Rich* has sold over sixty million copies worldwide and still sells about one million copies per year. Today a best seller is usually classified as a book that sells a hundred thousand copies. All of Hill's books have sold more than that, and most exceed a million copies. The more popular books today have what publishers refer to as a shelf life of one to two years (the length of time the book is in demand and remains in stock at major bookstores). Hill's *The Law of Success* has been in continuous publication since 1928, *Think and Grow Rich* since 1937, *Master Key to Riches* since 1945, *Success Through a Positive Mental Attitude* since 1960,

Grow Rich with Peace of Mind since 1967, and *You Can Work Your Own Miracles* since 1971. In other words, Hill's books sell better today than when he first wrote them.

—Don M. Green
   Executive Director
   The Napoleon Hill Foundation

PREFACE

How to Get the Most from Reading This Book

If you read Napoleon Hill's books, you will find several that include a section from the best seller *Success Through a Positive Mental Attitude*, which he wrote with W. Clement Stone. This article is called "How to Get the Most from Reading This Book."

In order to tap into the powers that are available to you, you must first be prepared to accept and apply the information.

The principles of success will work for you as they have for others, regardless of education, heredity, or environment. But if you take the belief you are destined to fail and that you cannot do anything to prevent it, you will surely fail. The choice is yours and yours alone.

The R2A2 Formula

The formula will tell you not only what to do but how to do it. If you are ready to use the R2A2 formula, here are two principles that will assure your success:

1. Recognize, Relate, Assimilate, and Apply principles, techniques, and methods from what you see, hear, read, and experience that can help you attain your goals. This is called the R2A2 formula.

The R2 stands for Recognize and Relate and A2 for Assimilate and Apply.

2. Direct your thoughts, control your emotions, and ordain your destiny by motivating yourself at will to achieve worthwhile goals.

In using the formula, keep your goals in mind and be ready to accept useful information.

As you read, concentrate on the meanings and words as they relate to your own goals. Read the material as if the author is writing to you.

As you read, underscore sentences or passages you feel are important to you.

Write in the margins when you are inspired with ideas that have potential benefit.

As you read and apply the R2A2 formula, remember that the second part of the formula is the most important point. This part many people hurry over and tend to avoid. These are the same people who make excuses or blame others for their lack of success. Without action the material will not be worth the price you pay for any self-help book.

—The Napoleon Hill Foundation

1

Your Social and Physical Heredity

*Y*our parents made you what you are, physically, but YOU can make yourself what you WILL, mentally.

You and every other human being are the sum total of just two things, heredity and environment.

You inherited certain physical tendencies and qualities from your parents. You inherited other tendencies and qualities from your grandparents, and from their parents.

The size of your body, the color of your hair and eyes, the texture of your skin, and certain other physical qualities of this nature you inherited; consequently, much of your physical makeup is a result of causes beyond your control.

Those qualities which were "wished" upon you, through your physical heredity, are, for the most part, qualities which you cannot change very materially.

However, it is another matter when you come to those qualities which you have developed out of your environment, or through what is called social heredity. You can change these qualities at will. Those which you developed before the age of ten years will, of course, be much harder to modify or change because they are deeply set, and you will find it hard to exercise sufficient willpower to change them.

Every sense impression which reaches your mind, from the moment of your birth, through any of the five senses, constitutes a part of your social heredity. The songs you sing or hear sung, the poems you read, the books you study, the sermons you listen to, the sights you see, all constitute a part of your social heredity.

Probably the most influential sources from which you absorb the tendencies which constitute your personality are these: first, the teachings which you receive at home, by your parents; secondly, your teachings at church or Sunday school; thirdly, your teachings in

3

public or private schools; fourthly, the daily newspapers and monthly magazines and your other reading.

You believe as you do, regarding every subject, as a result of the sense impressions which have reached your mind. Your belief may be false or correct, according to the soundness or unsoundness, truth or falsity, of those sense impressions.

If, in the process of your schooling, you have been taught how to think accurately; how to overcome prejudices which attach to race, creed, politics, and the like; how to see that nothing but facts impress themselves on your mind; how to keep away all sense impressions which do not arise out of truth, you are very fortunate, because you will be able to extract from your environment that which you can use to best advantage in developing your personality into exactly that which you want it to be.

Physical heredity is something that cannot be altered to any very great extent, but social heredity can be changed, and the new ideas can be made to take the place of the old, the truth to take the place of falsehood.

A small, weak body may be made to house a great mind by properly directing that mind through social heredity. On the other hand, a strong physical body may house a weak, inactive mind through the same cause. The mind is the sum total of all sense impressions which have reached the brain; therefore, you can see how important it is that these sense impressions arise out of truth, how important it is that they be kept free from prejudice, hatred, and the like.

The mind resembles a fertile field. It will produce a crop according to the nature of the seed that is sown in it, through the sense impressions which reach it.

By controlling four sources, the ideal of a nation or a people can be completely changed, or even supplanted by a new ideal, in one generation. These four sources are: (1) the home teachings, (2) the church teachings, (3) the public school teachings, and (4) the newspapers, magazines, and books.

Not Nearly Enough Blacks Understood This!

Through these four sources, any ideal, thought, or idea can be forced upon the child so indelibly that the results would be hard, if not impossible, to erase or change in afterlife.

Summarizing, we believe it worthwhile to repeat, in a few words, the two chief points made, namely:

First—Any ideal or habit which is intended to become a permanent fixture in a human being must be planted in his or her mind in early childhood, through the principle of social heredity. An idea so planted becomes a permanent part of that person and remains with him or her throughout life, excepting in very rare instances, where stronger influences than those which planted the idea tend to counteract or erase it. This principle is called social heredity, because it constitutes the medium through which the dominating qualities of a person are planted and developed out of all those sense impressions which reach the mind out of one's environment, through the five senses, as separate and distinct from those physical qualities which are inherited from the parents.

Second—One of the most important fundamental principles of psychology, through which the human mind functions, is the tendency of the mind to want that which is withheld, prohibited, or hard to acquire. The moment you remove an object out of reach of a person, that moment you set up in that person's mind a desire for that object. The moment you forbid a person to do a thing, that moment that person strongly desires to do the very thing it has been forbidden to do. The human mind resents being forced to do anything. *THIS!! To Blacks* Therefore, to plant an idea in a person's mind in such a way that it will remain there permanently, it must be so presented that the person welcomes it and readily accepts it. All competent salesmen are familiar with this principle, and practice the habit of so presenting the merits of their services, goods, or wares, that the prospective buyer is scarcely aware that the ideas he is forming are not originating in his own mind. X

These two principles are worthy of consideration by all who would become leaders in any worthwhile undertaking, because all successful leadership depends upon their use. Whether you are selling goods, practicing medicine or law, preaching sermons, writing books, teaching school, or managing commerce and industry, you will find your ability greatly augmented by studying, understanding, and using these two principles through which the human mind may be reached.

You are the sum total of just two factors, heredity and environment. You can't help how you were born, but you can build up your strong traits and overcome your weak ones. And you CAN change your environment, your thoughts, your purpose, your life aim. It's up to YOU; do you WANT to? Then you CAN.

2

Auto-Suggestion

HIS BOOKS!!

The term *auto-suggestion* simply means self-suggestion, suggestion which one deliberately makes to oneself.

James Allen, in his excellent little magazine, *As a Man Thinketh*, has given the world a fine lesson in auto-suggestion by having shown that a man may literally make himself over through this process of self-suggestion.

This lesson, like James Allen's magazine, is intended mainly as a means of stimulating men and women to the discovery and perception of the truth that "they themselves are makers of themselves," by virtue of the thoughts which they choose and encourage; that mind is the master weaver, both of the inner garment of character and the outer garment of circumstance; and that as they have hitherto woven in ignorance, pain, and grief, they may now weave in enlightenment and happiness.

This lesson is not a preachment, nor is it a treatise on morality or ethics. It is a scientific treatise through which the student may understand the reason why the first rung in the magic ladder to success was placed there, and how to make the principle back of that rung a part of his or her own working equipment with which to master life's most important economic problems.

This lesson is based upon the following facts:

1. Every movement of the human body is controlled and directed by thought, that is, by orders sent out from the brain, where the mind has its seat of government.
2. The mind is divided into two sections, one being called the conscious section (which directs our bodily activities while we are awake), and the other being called the subconscious section, which controls our bodily activity while we are asleep.

3. The presence of any thought or idea in one's conscious mind (and probably the same is true of thoughts and ideas in the subconscious division of the mind) tends to produce an "associated feeling" and to urge one to appropriate bodily activity in transforming the thought so held into physical reality. For example, one can develop courage and self-confidence by the use of the following, or some similar positive statement, or by holding the thought of this statement in one's mind constantly: "I believe in myself. I am courageous. I can accomplish whatever I undertake." This is called auto-suggestion.

We shall now proceed to give you the modus operandi through which the first step in the magic ladder to success can be appropriated and used. To begin with, search diligently until you find the particular work to which you wish to devote your life, taking care to see that you select that which will profit all who are affected by your activities. After you have decided what your life work is to be, write out a clear statement of it and then commit it to memory.

Several times a day, and especially just before going to sleep at night, repeat the words of this written description of your life work, and affirm to yourself that you are attracting to you the necessary forces, people, and material things with which to attain the object of your life work, or your definite aim in life.

Bear in mind that your brain is literally a magnet, and that it will attract to you other people who harmonize, in thought and in ideals, with those thoughts which dominate your mind and those ideals which are most deeply seated in you.

There is a law, which we may properly call the law of attraction, through the operation of which water seeks its level, and everything throughout the universe of like nature seeks its kind. If it were not for this law, which is as immutable as the law of gravitation which keeps the planets in their proper places, the cells out of which an oak tree grows might scamper away and become mixed with the cells out of which the poplar grows, thereby producing a tree that would be part poplar and part oak. But, such a phenomenon has never been heard of.

Following this law of attraction a little further, we can see how it works out among men and women. We know that successful, prosperous men of affairs seek the companionship of their own kind, while the down-and-outer seeks his kind, and this happens just as naturally as water flows downhill.

Like attracts like, a fact which is indisputable.

Then, if it is true that men are constantly seeking the companionship of those whose ideals and thoughts harmonize with their own, can you not see the importance of so controlling and directing your thoughts and ideals that you will eventually develop exactly the kind of "magnet" in your brain that you wish to serve as an attraction in drawing others to you?

If it is true that the very presence of any thought in your conscious mind has a tendency to arouse you to bodily, muscular activity that will correspond with the nature of the thought, can you not see the advantage of selecting, with care, the thoughts which you allow your mind to dwell upon?

Read these lines carefully, and think over and digest the meaning which they convey, because we are now laying the foundation for a scientific truth which constitutes the very foundation upon which all worthwhile human accomplishment is based. We are beginning, now, to build the roadway over which you will travel out of the wilderness of doubt, discouragement, uncertainty, and failure, and we want you to familiarize yourself with every inch of this road.

No one knows what thought is, but every philosopher and every man of scientific ability who has given any study to the subject is in accord with the statement that thought is a powerful form of energy which directs the activities of the human body, that every idea held in the mind through prolonged, concentrated thought takes on permanent form and continues to affect the bodily activities according to its nature, either consciously or unconsciously.

Auto-suggestion, which is nothing more or less than an idea held in the mind, through thought, is the only known principle through which one may literally make oneself over, after any pattern he or she may choose.

How to Develop Character through Auto-Suggestion

This brings us to an appropriate place at which to explain the method through which your author has literally made himself over during a period of approximately five years.

Before we go into these details, let us remind you of the common tendency of human beings to doubt that which they do not understand, and all that they cannot prove to their own satisfaction, either by similar experiences of their own or by observation.

Let us also remind you that this is no age for a Doubting Thomas. Your author, while a comparatively young man, has nevertheless seen the birth of some of the world's greatest inventions, the uncovering, as it were, of some of the so-called "hidden secrets" of nature. And he is well within the bounds of accuracy when he reminds you that during the last sixty years, science has lifted the curtains that separated us from the light of truth, and brought into use more tools of culture, development, and progress than had been discovered in all the previous history of the human race.

Within comparatively recent years, we have seen the birth of the incandescent electric light, the typesetting machine, the printing press, the x-ray, the telephone, the automobile, the airplane, the submarine, the wireless telegraphy, and myriad other organized forces which serve mankind and tend to separate him from the animal instincts of the dark ages out of which he has risen.

As these lines are being written, we are informed that Thomas A. Edison is at work on a contrivance which he believes will enable the departed spirits of men to communicate with us here on earth, if such a thing is possible. And if the announcement should come from East

Orange, New Jersey, tomorrow morning, that Edison has completed his machine and communicated with the spirits of departed men, this writer, for one, would not scoff at the statement. If we did not accept it as true until we had seen proof, we would at least hold an open mind on the subject, because we have witnessed enough of the "impossible" during the past thirty years to convince us that there is but little that is strictly impossible when the human mind sets itself to a task with that grim determination that knows no defeat.

If modern history informs us correctly, the best railroad men in the country scoffed at the idea that Westinghouse could stop a train by jamming air on the brakes, but those same men lived to see a law passed in the New York legislature compelling railroad companies to use this "foolish contrivance," and if it had not been for that law, the present speed of railroad trains and the safety with which we may travel would not be possible.

We are reminded to state, also, that had the illustrious Napoleon Bonaparte not scoffed at Robert Fulton's request for an interview, the French capital might be sitting on English soil today, and France might be the mistress over all of the British empire. Fulton sent word to Napoleon that he had invented a steam engine that would carry a boat against the wind, but Napoleon, never having seen such a contrivance, sent back word that he had no time to fool with cranks, and, furthermore, ships could not sail against the wind because ships never had been sailed that way.

Well within the memory of your author, a bill was introduced in Congress asking for an appropriation with which to experiment with an airplane which Samuel Pierpont Langley had worked out, but the appropriation was promptly denied, and Professor Langley was scoffed at as being an impractical dreamer and a "crank." No one had ever seen a man fly a machine in the air, and no one believed it could be done.

But, we are becoming a bit more liberal in our viewpoint concerning powers which we do not understand; at least those of us who do not wish to become the laughingstock of later generations are.

We felt impelled to remind you of these "impossibilities" of the past which turned out to be realities, before taking you behind the curtains of our own life and displaying, for your benefit, certain principles which we have reason to believe will be hard for the uninitiated to accept until they have been tried out and proved sound.

We will now proceed to unfold to you the most astonishing and, we might well say, the most miraculous experience of our entire past, an experience which is related solely for the benefit of those who are earnestly seeking ways and means to develop in themselves those qualities which constitute positive character.

When we first commenced to understand the principle of auto-suggestion several years ago, we adopted a plan for making practical use of it in developing certain qualities which we admired in certain men who are familiar characters in history, viz.:

Just before going to sleep at night, we made it a practice to close our eyes and see, in our imagination (please get this clearly fixed in your mind—what we saw was deliberately placed in our mind as instructions, or as a direct command to our subconscious mind, and as a blueprint for it to build by, through our imagination, and was in no way attributed to anything occult or in the field of uncharted phenomena) a large counsel table standing on the floor in front of us.

We then pictured, in our imagination, certain men seated around that table, those men from whose characters and lives we wished to appropriate certain qualities to be deliberately built into our own character, through the principle of auto-suggestion.

For example, some of the men whom we selected to take an imaginary place at the imaginary counsel table were Lincoln, Emerson, Socrates, Aristotle, Napoleon, Jefferson, Elbert Hubbard, the man from Galilee, and Henry Ward Beecher, the well-known English orator.

Our purpose was to impress our subconscious mind, through auto-suggestion, with the thought that we were developing certain qualities which we admired most in each of these and in other great men.

Night after night, for an hour or more at a time, we went through this imaginary meeting at the counsel table. As a matter of fact, we continue the practice to this day, adding a new character to the counsel table as often as we find someone from whom we wish to take certain qualities, through emulation.

From Lincoln, we wanted the qualities for which he was most noted—earnestness of purpose; a fair sense of justice toward all, both friends and foes alike; an ideal which had for its object the uplift of the masses, the common people; the courage to break precedents and to establish new ones when circumstances demanded it. All these qualities, which we had so much admired in Lincoln, we set out to develop in our own character while looking upon that imaginary counsel table, by actually commanding our subconscious mind to use the picture which it saw, at the counsel table, as a plan to build from.

We wished to take from Napoleon the quality of dogged persistency; we wanted his strategic ability to turn adverse circumstances to good account; we wanted his self-confidence and his wonderful ability to inspire and lead men; we wanted his ability to organize his own faculties and his fellow workers, because we knew that real power came only through intelligently organized and properly directed efforts.

From Emerson, we wanted that remarkably keen insight into the future for which he was noted. We wanted his ability to interpret nature's handwriting as it is manifested in flowing brooks, singing birds, laughing children, the blue skies, the starry heavens, the green grass, and the beautiful flowers. We wanted his ability to interpret human emotions, his ability to reason from cause to effect and, inversely, from effect back to cause.

We wanted Elbert Hubbard's power of words and his ability to interpret the trend of the times; we wanted his ability to combine words so they would convey the exact pictures of the thoughts we created; we wanted his ability to write in a rhythmic strain that would be unquestioned as to its meaning or its sincerity.

We wanted Beecher's magnetic power to grip the hearts of an audience, in public address, his ability to speak with force and conviction that moved an audience to laughter or to tears and made his listeners feel with him mirth and melody, sorrow, and good cheer.

As I saw those men sitting there before me, seated around the imaginary counsel table, I would direct my attention to each of them for a few minutes, saying to myself that I was developing those qualities which I aimed to appropriate from the character before me.

If you have tears of grief to shed for me, on account of my ignorance in going through this imaginary role of character building, get ready to shed them now. If you have words of condemnation to utter against my practice, utter them now. If you have a feeling of cynicism which seems to strive for expression in the nature of a scowling face, give expression to it now, because I am about to relate something which ought to, and probably will, cause you to stop, look, and reason!

Up until the time that I began these imaginary counsel meetings, I had made many attempts at public speaking, all of which had been dismal failures. The very first speech I attempted to deliver after a week of this practice, I so impressed my audience that I was invited back for another talk on the same subject, and from that day until the time of the writing of these lines, I have been constantly improving.

Last year, the demand for my services as a public speaker became so universal that I toured the greater portion of the United States, speaking before the leading clubs, civic organizations, schools, and specially arranged meetings.

In the city of Pittsburgh, during the month of May, 1920, I delivered the "Magic Ladder to Success" before the Advertising Club. In my audience were some of the leading businessmen of the United States, officials from the Carnegie Steel Company, the H.J. Heinz Pickle Company, the Joseph Horne Department Store, and other great industries of the city. These men were analytical men. Many of them were college and university graduates. They were men who knew when they heard something that was sound. At the close of my address, they gave me what several members of the audience afterward told me was the greatest ovation ever given a speaker before that club. Shortly after my return from Pittsburgh, I received a medal from the Associated Advertising Clubs of the World, in memory of that event, engraved as follows: "In Appreciation of Napoleon Hill, May 20, 1920."

Please do not make the mistake of interpreting the foregoing as an outburst of egotism. I am giving you facts, names, dates, and places, and I am doing this only for the purpose of showing you that the quality which I so greatly admired in Henry Ward Beecher I had actually commenced to develop in myself. This quality was developed, around the imaginary counsel table, with my eyes shut, while looking at an imaginary figure of Mr. Beecher seated as a member of my imaginary board of counselors.

The principle through which I developed this ability was auto-suggestion. I filled my mind so full of the thought that I would equal, and even excel, Beecher before I stopped that no other result could have been the outcome.

Nor is this the end of my narrative—a narrative which, by the way, the hundreds of thousands who know me now, located in nearly every city, town, and hamlet throughout the United States, can corroborate! I began, immediately, to supplant intolerance with tolerance; I began to emulate the immortal Lincoln in those wonderful qualities of justice toward all, friend and foe alike. New power began to come, not alone to my spoken words, but to my pen as well, and I saw, as plainly as I could see the sun on a clear day, the steady development of that ability to express myself with force and conviction by the written word, which I had so much admired in Elbert Hubbard.

In speaking of this very point, not many months ago, Mr. Myers, an official of the Morris Packing Company of Chicago, made the remark that my editorials in *Hill's Golden Rule Magazine* reminded him very forcefully of the late Elbert Hubbard, and added that he had just stated to one of his associates a few days previously that I was not only big enough to fill Elbert Hubbard's shoes, but that I had already outgrown them.

Again, I remind you not to brush these facts aside lightly, or to charge them to egotism. If I write as well as Hubbard, it is because I have aspired to do so, first having deliberately made use of auto-suggestion to charge my mind with the aim and purpose of not only equaling him, but of excelling him if possible.

> There will be no lasting peace on earth until the human race is taught that physical conflict cannot decide a moral issue.

I am not unmindful of the fact that the display of egotism is an unpardonable weakness, in either a writer or a speaker, and no one more readily denounces such shallowness of mind than this writer. However, I must also remind you that it is not always a sign of egotism when a writer refers to his own personal experiences for the purpose of giving his readers authentic data on a given subject. Sometimes it requires courage to do so. In this particular case, I would refrain from the free use of the personal pronoun "I" which has so frequently crept into this narrative, were it not for the fact that to do so would take away much of the value of my work. I am relating these personal experiences solely because I know they are authentic, believing, as I do, that it is preferable to run the risk of being classed as egotistical rather than use a hypothetical illustration of the principle of auto-suggestion or write in the third person.

༆

The Value of a Definite Aim in Life

Your author gives the same care and attention to the details of his definite aim in life as he would to the plans of a skyscraper if he contemplated building one. Your achievement in life will be no more definite than were the plans by which you attained your objective.

A little more than a year and a half prior to the writing of these lines, I revised my written statement of my definite aim in life, changing the paragraph headed "Income" to read as follows:

I will earn $100,000 a year because I will need this sum to carry on the educational program which I have outlined for my School of Business Economics.

Within less than six months from the day that I made this change in the wording of my definite aim in life, I was approached by the head of a corporation who offered me a business connection at a salary of $105,200 a year, the $5,200 being intended to cover my traveling expenses to and from the place of employment, which was a long distance from Chicago, leaving the amount agreed upon for the salary exactly the amount that I had indicated in my written statement of my definite aim.

I accepted this offer, and in less than five months, I had created an organization and other assets for the concern that employed me that were estimated to be worth over $20 million. I refrain from mentioning names only for the reason that I feel duty-bound to state that my employer found a loophole through which he defrauded me out of the $100,000 salary agreed upon.

There are two outstanding facts to which I would direct your attention, namely:

First, I was offered exactly the amount which I had set out in my definite aim as being the amount I intended to earn during the ensuing year.

Secondly, I actually earned the amount (and, in fact, many times more than earned it) even though I did not collect it.

Now, please go back to the wording of my declaration that I would "earn $100,000 a year" and ask yourself the question, "What would have been the difference, if any, had the declaration read, 'I will earn and RECEIVE $100,000 a year'?"

Frankly, I do not know whether it would have made any difference in results if I had so worded my definite aim. On the other hand, it might have made a great deal of difference.

Who is wise enough to either affirm or deny the statement that there is a law of the universe through which we attract to us that which we believe in life that we can attain through this same law; that we receive that which we demand, providing the demand is possible of attainment and is based upon equity, justice, and a clearly defined plan.

I am convinced that it is impossible to defeat the purpose of a person who organizes his or her efforts. Out of such organization, your author has attained, with astounding speed, the position in life to which he aspired, and he knows anyone else can do the same.

Service and sacrifice are passwords to the very highest success.

In my public addresses during the past twelve months, I suppose I have stated it as my opinion, at least a thousand times, that the person who takes the time to build a definite plan that is sound and equitable, that benefits all whom it affects, and then develops the self-confidence to carry it through to completion cannot be defeated.

I have never been accused of being overly credulous or superstitious. I have never been impressed very much by so-called miracles, but I am compelled to admit that I have seen the working out, in my own evolution during the past twenty-odd years, certain principles which have produced seemingly miraculous results. I have watched the development and unfoldment of my own mind, and while I ordinarily am not very deeply impressed by any "miracle," the cause of which I cannot trace, I must admit that much has happened in the development of my own mind which I cannot trace back to original cause.

This much I do know, however; I know that my outward bodily action invariably harmonizes with and corresponds to the nature of the thoughts which dominate my mind, the thoughts which I permit to drift into my mind, or those which I deliberately place there with the intention of giving them domination over my bodily activities.

My own experience has proved conclusively that character need not be a matter of chance! Character can be built to order just the same as a house can be built to correspond to a set of previously drawn up plans. My own experience has proved conclusively that a man can rebuild his character in a remarkably short length of time, ranging all the way from a few weeks to a few years, depending upon the determination and the desire with which he goes at a task.

Happiness is the only good. The place to be happy is here. The time to be happy is now. The way to be happy is to help make others so.

—**ROBERT G. INGERSOLL**

A few months before I began these lessons on applied psychology, I had an experience which gained considerable attention among the interested parties here in the city of Chicago. As I was getting off an elevator in the retail department of A.C. McClurg & Company (Chicago's largest book and stationery house), the elevator man allowed the elevator door to slip and catch me between the door and the wall of the elevator. Besides causing me great pain, the accident tore the sleeve of my coat, damaging it to what looked like beyond repair.

I reported the accident to the store manager, a Mr. Ryan, who very courteously informed me that I would be reimbursed for the damage done. After a time, the insurance company sent out its agent, looked my coat over, and paid me $40 for the damage. After the settlement was made and all parties concerned were satisfied, I took the coat to my tailor, and he made such a neat repair that one could not tell where the coat was torn. The tailor's bill was $2.

I had $38 that did not belong to me, yet the insurance company was satisfied, mainly, I suppose, because it got off by paying for less than half the cost of a new suit. A.C. McClurg & Company was satisfied because my damage had been made good by their insurance company, and the affair had cost them nothing.

But I was not satisfied!

There were many purposes for which I could use that $38. Legally, it belonged to me, I was in possession of it, and there was no one to ever question my right to it or the means by which I acquired it.

Had the insurance company known that the suit could have been so neatly repaired, it probably would have demurred against paying such a large bill, but the question of how the repair would turn out was one that could not be determined in advance.

I argued with my conscience for that $38, but it would not permit me to keep it, so I finally compromised by handing back half of the amount and keeping the other half, on the theory that I had lost considerable time in bringing about the adjustment, and also on the theory that the repair might show up the defective part of the garment later on. I had to stretch matters considerably in my own favor before I felt justified in keeping more than the actual cost of the repairs.

When I handed back the money, the representative of McClurg & Company suggested that I just keep the money and forget it, to which I replied, "That's just the trouble; I would like to keep it, but I couldn't *forget* it!"

There was a sound reason why I handed back that $20. That reason had nothing to do with ethics or honesty. It had nothing to do with the rights of A.C. McClurg & Company or of the insurance company that was protecting McClurg & Company. In arriving at my decision to hand back the money, I never took into consideration either McClurg or the insurance company. They were entirely out of the transaction because they were satisfied. What I really took into consideration was my own character, knowing as I did that every transaction was influencing my moral fiber, and that character is nothing more or less than the sum total of one's habits and ethical conduct. I knew that I could no more afford to keep that $20 without first having earned the right to it than an apple merchant could afford to place a rotten apple in a barrel of sound ones prior to storing the barrel away for the winter.

a) Making Many..

I gave back the $20 because I wanted to convince *myself* that no material could find its way into my character, with my knowledge, except that which I knew to be sound. I gave back the money because it offered a splendid opportunity for me to test myself and ascertain whether or not I possessed that brand of honesty which prompts a man to be honest for the sake of expedience, or that deeper, nobler, and more worthy brand which prompts a man to be honest that he may grow stronger and more able to render his fellowmen service that grows out of a desire to be all that he tells the other man to be.

I am convinced that if a man's plans are based upon sound economic principles; if they are fair and just to all whom they affect; and if the man, himself, can throw behind those plans the dynamic force of character and belief in self that grows out of the transactions which have always satisfied his own conscience, he will ride on to success, with and by the aid of a tremendous current of force which no power on earth can stop, nay, a force which but few can correctly interpret or understand.

DEEP!!

Power is organized knowledge that is controlled and directed to ends that are based upon justice and equity to all who are affected. There are two classes of human power. One is attained through the organization of the individual faculties, and the other is attained through the organization of individuals who work harmoniously to a common end. There can be no power except through intelligently directed organization.

You cannot organize your individual faculties except through the use of the principle of auto-suggestion, for the simple reason that you cannot vitalize or give dynamic force to your faculties, your emotions, your intellect, your reasoning powers, or your bodily functions, without collecting all of these together, co-relating them, and working them into a plan.

No plan, great or small, can be developed in your mind except through the principle of auto-suggestion.

DEEP!!

The mind resembles a rich garden spot in that it will grow a crop of outward, physical, bodily activity which corresponds exactly to the nature of the thoughts that dominate the mind, whether those thoughts are deliberately placed there and held until they take root and grow, or merely drift in as so many stragglers, taking up their abode without invitation.

There is no escape from the effects of one's dominating thoughts. There is no possibility of thinking of failure, poverty, and discouragement and at the same time enjoying success, wealth, and courage. You can choose that which holds the attention of your mind; therefore, you can control the development of your character, which, in turn, helps to determine the character of people whom you will attract to you. Your own mind is the magnet which attracts to you those with whom you associate most closely, the station in life you hold. Therefore, it is within your province to magnetize that mind only with thoughts that will attract the sort of people with whom you wish to associate and the station in life to which you are willing to attain.

Auto-suggestion is the very foundation upon which and through which an attractive personality is built, for the reason that character grows to resemble the dominating thoughts that help in the mind, and these, in turn, control the action of the body.

When you make use of the principle of auto-suggestion, you are painting a picture or drawing a plan for your subconscious mind to work by. After you learn how to properly concentrate or fix your attention on this process of plan building, you can reach your subconscious mind instantly, and it will put your plans into action.

Beginners must repeat over and over again the outline of their plans before the subconscious mind will take over the plans and transform them into reality. Therefore, be not discouraged if you do not get results on the spur of the moment. Only those who have attained mastership can reach and direct their subconscious mind instantaneously.

In closing this lesson, let me remind you that back of this principle of auto-suggestion is one important thing which you must not overlook, and that is strong, deeply seated, highly emotional desire. Desire is the very beginning of mind operation. You can create in the physical reality practically anything you can desire with deep, vitalized emotion.

Deep desire is the beginning of all human accomplishments. Auto-suggestion is merely the principle through which that desire is communicated to your subconscious mind. Probably you do not have to go outside of your own experience to prove that it is comparatively easy to acquire that which one strongly desires.

Next time, we will take up the subject of suggestion and show how to use your dynamic, attractive personality after you have developed it through auto-suggestion. Suggestion is the very foundation of all successful salesmanship.

3

Suggestion

*I*n the previous lesson, we learned the meaning of auto-suggestion and the principles through which it may be used. Auto-suggestion means self-suggestion. We now come to our next principle of psychology, which is as follows:

Suggestion is a principle of psychology through the correct use of which we may influence, direct, and control the minds of others. It is the chief principle used in advertising and salesmanship. It is the principle through which Mark Antony swayed the Roman mob in that wonderful speech outlined in "The Psychology of Salesmanship" (by Napoleon Hill).

Suggestion differs from auto-suggestion in only one way—we use it to influence the minds of others, while we use auto-suggestion in influencing our own minds.

Suggestion is one of the most subtle and powerful principles of psychology. Science has proved that through the destructive use of this principle, life may be actually extinguished, while all manner of disease may be eliminated through its constructive use.

On numerous occasions, I have demonstrated the remarkable power of suggestion in the following manner, before my classes in applied psychology:

Taking a two-ounce bottle labeled "Oil of Peppermint," I make a brief explanation that I wish to demonstrate the power of smell. Then, holding the bottle in front of my class so all may see it, I explain that it contains oil of peppermint, and that a few drops of it poured on a handkerchief which I hold in my hand will penetrate the farthest end of the room in about forty seconds. I then uncork the bottle and pour a few drops on my handkerchief, at the same time turning my face out of shape to indicate that I have had too strong a draught of the odor. I then request the members of the class to hold up their hands as fast as they get the first whiff of the odor of the peppermint.

The hands begin to go up rapidly until, in some instances, seventy-five percent of the class have their hands up.

I then take the bottle, drink the contents slowly and complacently, and explain that it contained *pure water*! No one smelled any peppermint at all! It was an olfactory illusion, produced entirely through the principle of suggestion.

In the little town where I was raised there lived an old lady who constantly complained that she feared death from cancer. As long as I can remember, she nursed this habit. She was sure that every little imaginary ache or pain was the beginning of her long-expected cancer. I have seen her place her hand on her breast and have heard her say, "Oh, I am sure I have cancer growing here." When complaining of this imaginary disease, she always placed her hand on her left breast, the spot where she believed the cancer would attack her.

As I write this lesson, news comes that this old lady has died of cancer on the left breast, in the very spot where she placed her hand when she complained of her fears!

If suggestion will actually turn healthy body cells into parasites out of which a cancer grows, can you not imagine what it will do in eliminating diseased body cells and replacing them with healthy ones?

If an audience of people can be made to smell oil of peppermint when a bottle of plain water is uncorked, through the principle of suggestion, can you not see what remarkable possibilities there are for constructively using this principle in every legitimate task you perform?

Some years ago, a criminal was condemned to death. Before his execution, an experiment was performed on him which conclusively proved that through the principle of suggestion, death could actually be produced. This criminal was brought to the guillotine, his head placed under the knife after he had been blindfolded, and a heavy board was dropped on his neck, producing a shock similar to that of the knife of the guillotine. Warm water was poured gently and allowed to trickle slowly down his neck, to imitate warm blood. In seven minutes, the doctors pronounced the criminal dead. His imagination, through the principle of suggestion, had actually turned the sharp-edged board into a guillotine blade and stopped his heart from beating.

Every single case of the healing of disease by practitioners of "mental healing" is accomplished through the principle of sugges-tion. We learn from good authority that many physicians are using fewer drugs and more mental suggestion in their practice. Two physicians who are members of my own family supplied me with the information that they use more "bread pills" than they did a few years ago. One of these physicians told me of a case in which one of his patients was relieved of a violent headache in a very few minutes by taking what the patient believed to be aspirin, but which was, in reality, a white flour tablet.

Hypnotism operates entirely through the principle of suggestion. Quite contrary to the general belief, a person cannot be hypnotized without his consent. The truth is that it is the subject's own mind and not the mind of the operator or hypnotist that produces the phenomenon which we call hypnotism.

All the operator can possibly do toward hypnotizing a person is to "neutralize" the subject's conscious mind and then place in his subconscious mind whatever suggestions are desired. By "neutraliz-ing" the mind, we have reference to the performance of overcoming or rendering powerless the conscious mind of the subject. We will come back to this subject again, and explain some of the methods through which the conscious mind may be rendered impotent or inoperative, but first let us understand the method through which hypnotism is produced, as described in the words of a hypnotist, as follows:

After talking sympathetically with the subject, sometimes for an hour or two, in regard to the failing he wishes removed, thoroughly acquainting myself with his dominant propensities or

controlling thought, and, above all, securing his confidence, I ask him to assume a comfortable reclining position on a lounge, and then continue a soothing conversation along lines like the following with a view to producing a monotonous impression on eye and ear.

"I wish you would look at this diamond (or select any convenient object in line of vision) in a dreamy, listless manner and a blank, expressionless stare, thinking of nothing, not concentrating your mind or focusing your eye upon it, but relaxing the ocular muscles so that it Has a confused outline. Abstain from that effort with the eyes that you are accustomed to make in order to see a near object distinctly. Rather, look through the stone and past it, as you look at a dead tree standing between you and a distant view you are contemplating.

"Make no effort, for there is nothing you can do to encourage the approach of the favorable mind state. Do not wonder what is going to happen, for nothing is going to happen. Do not be apprehensive, or suspicious, or distrustful. Do not desire that anything shall take place, nor watch to see what may occur—nor seek to analyze what is going on in your mind. You are as negative, indolent, and indifferent as you can be without trying to be.

"You are to expect the familiar signs of the approach of sleep, and they are all associated with the failure of the senses and the standstill of the brain—heavy eyelids, reluctant ears, muscles and skin indifferent to stimuli of temperature,

humidity, penetrability, etc. Already that delightful sensation of 'drowsiness' weights your eyelids down and steeps your senses in 'forgetfulness,' and you yield to the impulse as the curtains are dropped between you and the outside world of color and light.

"And your ear seeks to share in the rest of the senses. As darkness is the sleep of the eye, so is silence that of the ear; and your ear secures silence by deadening itself to sound impressions. The sound of my voice loses interest for you, and force and decisiveness seem to be receding into a mysterious remoteness. A grateful sense of surrender to some pleasing influence which you cannot resist, and would not if you could, descends upon you and enwraps your whole body in its beneficent embrace, and you are physically happy. Refreshing sleep has come to you."

From the foregoing, you have clearly seen that the hypnotist's first task is to render impotent the conscious mind. (By "conscious mind," we have reference to that division of the mind which we use when we are awake.) After the conscious mind has been "neutralized" or rendered inoperative, partly or in whole, the hypnotist manipulates his subject through suggestions direct to the subject's subconscious mind. The subconscious mind does whatever it is told. It asks no questions, but acts upon the sense impressions which reach it through the five senses. Reason, operating through the conscious mind, stands a sentinel during the waking hours, guarding the gateways of sight, smell, taste, touch, and hearing, but the moment we go to sleep or become semi-conscious from any cause, this guard becomes inoperative.

There are varying degrees of hypnotism to which a person may be subjected, through the principle of suggestion. The professional

So ReaL!.. Fur Black folks

hypnotist, performing on the stage, usually gains complete control of his subjects' minds, causing them to engage in all sorts of undignified and inconsistent antics. There is a much slighter degree of hypnotism to which a person may be subjected, and through which he may be controlled without his being conscious of the fact. It is to this more "invisible" or unnoticeable degree of hypnotism that we wish to direct your attention, because it is the degree most commonly practiced by the nonprofessional on those whom he chooses to control or influence.

THIS

(Whether the subject is under complete hypnotic control or only partly influenced, there is one condition which must exist in his mind, and that is credulousness. The hypnotist, whether he is of the professional or nonprofessional type, must first place this subject in a state of abnormal credulousness before he can direct or control his mind.)

In other words, before any mind can be influenced through suggestion, it must first be "neutralized." This brings us back to the question of describing the methods through which the mind may be "neutralized."

In other words, we shall now show you how to make practical application of the principle of suggestion, first warning you, however, that it will bring you success or failure, happiness or woe, according to the use which you make of it!

I can best describe what is meant by "neutralizing" the mind by relating a case which covers the meaning very concretely. A few years ago, the police arrested a gang of notorious crooks who were operating "clairvoyant" or "fortune telling" parlors in the city of Chicago. The head of this chain of fake shops was a man by the name of Bertsche. The scheme was to meet superstitious, credulous people of means who came to these shops to have their fortunes told and, by a series of mind manipulations which I will describe, to defraud them out of their money.

The "seeress" or woman in charge of one of these fake fortune telling shops would learn the secrets of her patrons, the extent of their finances, of what their wealth consisted, and all other necessary data. Getting this information was a simple matter since the business of the fortune telling shop is to advise people in matters of business, love, health, etc. Suitable victims were located in this manner and the information gathered and passed on to the head of the "clairvoyant trust," Mr. Bertsche.

At the most opportune time, the "seeress" would advise her victim to consult with some businessman who could be trusted to be free from prejudices that attach to "scheming blood relations," at the same time saying that the victim would soon meet such a man. Sure enough, pretty soon Mr. Bertsche "happens" to be in the fake fortune telling shop consulting "Madam Seeress" on matters of investment and business in general, and, by "mere accident," the victim is introduced to him.

"He is a man of great wealth," so the victim is told in confidence by the "seeress." She further confides the information that he is a "big-hearted" man who loves to help other people succeed in business. Mr. Bertsche is faultlessly dressed and looks the part of wealth and prosperity. He meets the victim, chats pleasantly, and hurries away to meet an important engagement with "Mr. Morganbilt."

The next time the victim comes to the fake fortune telling shop, he or she (they duped both sexes with equal success) will likely see Mr. Bertsche "just leaving to keep another appointment with rich Mr. Vandermorgan." He hurries right on out, apparently showing but little deference to the victim. This performance is repeated several times, until the victim gets over his or her "gun-shyness" and begins to feel that Mr. Bertsche is a busy man, and that he has but little time to devote to others.

Finally, after the victim has been carried through the first degree of mind manipulation and made to feel that a dinner invitation from Mr. Bertsche would be a highly honored privilege, like as not such an invitation will be extended. The victim will be escorted to the most exclusive club, or the finest café, and treated to a dinner that will cost more than a whole week's living expenses would ordinarily cost. The bill is paid by the host, Mr. Bertsche, who has been introduced as "Judge" somebody or other, and who apparently is rolling in money and running to get away from its accumulation.

In Mr. Bertsche's inside pocket is a card index showing in detail every weakness, every eccentricity, every peculiarity of the victim, who has been accurately analyzed and charged. If he is a dog fancier, that fact is ascertained and charged. If he loves horses, that, too, is known.

The game has commenced! If, for example, the victim likes horseback riding, the affable, rich, and well-kept Mr. Bertsche will see to it that one of his thoroughbreds is placed at the victim's disposal. If the victim likes automobiling, affable Mr. Bertsche's Packard will be waiting at the door ready to accommodate.

The form of entertainment will vary according to the tastes of the victim, and the expense of it is always borne by the now "trusted friend," Mr. Bertsche. This line of procedure is kept up until the victim's mind is *completely neutralized*! In other words, until the victim entirely ceases to feel suspicious of anything that may happen or anything that may be said or even suggested. The affable Mr. Bertsche has completely wormed himself into his victim's confidence, all this coming about by the merest "accidental meeting," of course. In some cases, Mr. Bertsche would "play his victim" for six months before reaching the opportune moment at which to strike, and often the cost of the entertainment and the "settings of the stage" would mount up into the hundreds and even into the thousands of dollars.

According to the reports of the cases which came to light, some of Bertsche's victims gave up as much as $50,000 by "investing" funds in worthless enterprises, upon his recommendation, or upon his "casual" remark that he had funds invested in such and such a proposition that were paying him handsome returns. On one occasion, he casually displayed a "dividend" check for $10,000 which he had just received from an investment of only $20,000 in some fake corporation. Mind you, he was too clever to try to persuade his victims to invest in one of these fake enterprises—he knew human nature too well for that—he merely was a bit "careless" in letting information out now and then which the victim could easily pick up and make use of.

Suggestion is more effective than out-and-out demand or request.

Subtle suggestion is a wonderful power, and "wealthy" Mr. Bertsche knew exactly how to apply it. On one occasion, it is said that his victim, an old woman, became so credulous that she actually drew a large sum of money out of the bank, took it to Mr. Bertsche, and tried vainly to get him to take it and invest it for her. He turned her away, telling her that he had surplus money of his own which he would like to put to work, and there was no opening just at that time. The reason the affable Mr. Bertsche turned the lady away was that he was playing her for larger stakes. He knew how much money she had, and he intended to get it all, so the lady was agreeably surprised a few days later when Mr. Bertsche telephoned her that, through a very special friend of his, she "might possibly get the chance" to invest in a certain block of very valuable stock, provided that she could take the whole block. He couldn't guarantee that she could get it, but she might try. She did! Her money was reposing in Bertsche's inside pocket an hour afterward.

We have gone into these details to show you exactly what is meant by rendering the mind "neutral." All that is needed to neutralize the mind and prepare it to accept and act under any suggestion is extreme credulousness, or credulousness greater than that normally exercised by the subject. Obviously, there are thousands of ways of neutralizing a person's mind and preparing it to receive any seed which we wish to plant there through suggestion. It is not necessary to try to enumerate them, because you can draw from your own experience all that you will need to give you a practical working knowledge of the principle and its method of application.

In some cases, it may require months in which to prepare a person's mind to receive that which you wish to place there, through suggestion. In other cases, a few minutes or even a few seconds may be sufficient. You may as well accept it as a positive fact, however, that you cannot influence the mind of a person who is antagonistic toward you, or who has not implicit faith and confidence in you. The very first step to be taken, therefore, whether you are preaching a sermon, selling merchandise, or pleading a case before a jury, is to gain the confidence of whomever you wish to influence.

Read that remarkable speech of Marc Antony at the burial of Caesar, in Shakespeare's works, and you will see how a hostile mob was completely disarmed by Marc Antony through the use of the very same principle that we are describing in this lesson.

Let us analyze the beginning of this wonderful speech, for herein may be found a lesson in applied psychology that is second to none. The mob has heard Brutus state his reason for killing Caesar and has been swayed by him. Marc Antony, Caesar's friend, now comes onstage to present his side of the case. The mob is against him to start with. Furthermore, it is expecting him to attack Brutus. But Marc Antony, the clever psychologist that he is, does nothing of the sort. Says he, "Friends, Romans, Countrymen, lend me your ears; I come to bury Caesar, not to praise him."

The mob had expected that he had come to praise his friend Caesar (which he had), but he had no notion of trying to do so until the minds of the mob had been neutralized and prepared to receive favorably that which he intended to say. Had the plan upon which Marc Antony's speech was built been reversed, and had he referred sneeringly to Brutus as being an "honorable" man in the beginning, he would likely have been assassinated by the mob.

One of the most able and successful lawyers I ever saw makes use of the same psychology that Marc Antony employed, in addressing a jury. I once heard him address a jury with words which led me to believe, for a few minutes, that he was either drunk or that he had suddenly lost his reason.

He began by extolling the virtues of his opponents, and apparently he was helping them establish their case against his own client. He began by saying, "Now, gentlemen of the jury, I do not wish to startle you, but there are many points in connection with this case that are against my client," and he proceeded to call attention to every one of them. (These points, of course, had been brought out by opposing counsel anyway.)

After he had gone along this line for a time, he suddenly stopped and, with deep dramatic effect, said, "But—that is what the other side says about this case. Now that we know what their contentions are, let us turn to the other side of the case." From that point on, this lawyer played upon the minds of that jury as a violinist would play upon the strings of his instrument, and within fifteen minutes, he had half of them in tears. At the end of his speech, he dropped into his seat, apparently overcome with emotion. The jury filed out and, in less than half an hour, returned with a verdict for his client.

Had this lawyer started out by stating the weak side of his opponent's case and urging upon the jury the merits of his own case too soon, he would undoubtedly have suffered defeat. But, as I afterwards learned, this lawyer was a close student of Shakespeare. He made use of the Marc Antony psychology in nearly all of his cases, and it is said that he lost fewer cases than any other lawyer in the community in which he practiced.

This same principle is used by the successful salesman, who not only refrains from "knocking" his competitor, but actually goes out of his way to speak highly of him. No person ought to consider himself a finished salesman until he has mastered the Marc Antony psychology and learned how to apply it. This speech is one of the greatest lessons in salesmanship ever written. If a salesman loses a sale, the chances are about ninety-nine to one that he lost it because of lack of proper preparation of the prospective buyer's mind. He spent too much time trying to "close" the sale and not enough time "preparing" the buyer's mind. He tried to reach his climax too soon. The successful salesman must prepare the buyer's mind to receive suggestions without either questioning or resisting them!

The human mind is an intricate affair. One of its characteristics is the fact that all impressions which reach the subconscious division are recorded in groups which harmonize and which are apparently closely related. When one of these impressions is called into the conscious mind, there is a tendency to recall all of the others with it. For example, one single act or word that causes a feeling of doubt to arise in a person's mind is sufficient to call into his conscious mind all of his experiences which caused him to be doubtful. Through the law of association, all similar emotions, experiences, or sense impressions which reach the mind are recorded together, so that the recalling of one has a tendency to bring out the others.

Just as a small pebble will, when thrown into the water, start a chain of ripples that will rapidly multiply, the subconscious mind has a tendency to bring into consciousness all of the associated or closely related emotions or sense impressions which it has stored, when one of them is aroused. To arouse a feeling of doubt in a person's mind has a tendency to bring to the surface every doubt-building experience that person ever had. That is why successful salesmen endeavor to keep away from subjects that may arouse the buyer's "chain of doubt impressions." The able salesman has long since learned that to "knock" a competitor may result in bringing to the buyer's conscious mind certain negative emotions which may make it impossible for the salesman to "neutralize" his mind.

This principle applies to and controls every emotion and every sense impression that is lodged in the human mind. Take the feeling of fear, for example; the moment we permit one single emotion that is related to fear to reach the conscious mind, it calls with it all of its unsavory relations. A feeling of courage cannot claim the attention of our conscious mind while a feeling of fear is there. One must supplant the other. They cannot become roommates, because they do not harmonize. Every thought held in the conscious mind has a tendency to draw to it every other harmonious or related thought. You see, therefore, that those feelings, thoughts, and emotions which claim the attention of the conscious mind are backed by a regular army of supporting soldiers who stand ready to aid them in their work.

Place in a man's mind, through the principle of suggestion, the ambition to succeed in any undertaking, and you will see that man's

NEVER ALLOW THIS DARRYL!!
FROM ANYONE!!

THIS!!

latent ability aroused and his powers automatically increased. Plant in your boy's mind, through the principle of suggestion, the ambition to become a successful lawyer, doctor, engineer, or businessman, and if you keep away all counter-influences, you will see that boy reach the desired goal.

THIS

It is much easier to influence a child through suggestion than it is an adult, for the reason that in the mind of a child, there are not so many opposing influences to break down in the process of "neutralizing" the mind, and he is naturally more credulous than an older person.

In the principle of suggestion lies the great roadway to success in the organization and management of men. The superintendent, foreman, manager, or president of an organization who fails to understand and use this principle is depriving himself of the most powerful force through which to influence his men.

One of the most able and efficient managers that I ever knew was a man who never criticized one of his men. To the contrary, he constantly reminded them of how well they were doing! He made a practice of going among his men, stopping here and there to lay a hand on a man's shoulder and compliment him on the manner in which he was improving. It made no difference how poor a man's work was, this manager never reprimanded him. By constantly placing in the minds of his men, through the principle of suggestion, the thought that "they are improving," they caught the suggestion and were promptly and effectively influenced by it.

One day, this manager stopped by the workbench of a man whose record showed that his work was decreasing in quantity. The man was working on piecework. Laying his hand on this man's shoulder, he said, "Jim, I believe you are doing much better work than you were last week. You seem to be setting the other boys a lively pace. I'm glad to see this. Go to it, my boy, I'm with you to the end!"

This happened about one o'clock in the afternoon. That night, Jim's tally sheet showed that he had actually turned out twenty-five percent more work than he had done the day before!

If any man doubts that wonders can be performed through the principle of suggestion, it is because he has not given enough time to the study of the principle to understand it.

Have you not noticed that the friendly, enthusiastic, "breezy," talkative, "hail fellow well met" type of person gets along better than the more sedate as a leader of men in any undertaking? Surely you must have noticed that the grouchy, sullen, noncommunicative sort of person never succeeds in attracting people to him or in influencing them to do his bidding. The principle of suggestion is at work constantly whether we are aware of it or not. Through this principle, which is as immutable as the law of gravitation, we are constantly influencing those around us and causing them to absorb the spirit which we radiate and to reflect this spirit in everything they do.

Surely you have noticed how one disgruntled person will cast a shadow of discontent over those with whom he associates. One agitator or troublemaker can disrupt a whole force of workmen and soon render their services worthless. On the other hand, one cheerful, optimistic, loyal, and enthusiastic person will influence a whole organization and inoculate it with the spirit which he manifests.

Whether we know it or not, we are constantly passing on to others our own emotions, feelings, and thoughts. In most instances, we are doing this unconsciously. In our next lesson, we shall show you how to make conscious use of this great principle of suggestion, through the law of retaliation.

In the next lesson, we shall show you how to "neutralize" the mind and how to get people to work in complete harmony with you, through application of the principle of suggestion.

In this lesson, you have learned something about one of the major principles of psychology, which is suggestion. You have learned that there are two steps to be taken in manipulating this principle, as follows:

First, you must "neutralize" the subject's mind before you can influence it through thoughts which you wish to plant there, through suggestion.

Second, to "neutralize" a mind, you must produce in it a state of credulousness greater than that normally maintained by the subject.

Fortunate is the person who controls his egotism and his desire for self-expression to the extent that he is willing to pass his own ideas on to others without insisting on reminding them as to the source of those ideas. The man who begins his statement with "As you of course know, Mr. Smith," instead of "Let me tell you something you do not know, Mr. Smith," is a salesman who knows how to make use of the principle of suggestion.

One of the cleverest and most able salesmen I ever knew was a man who rarely took credit for any information that he passed on to his prospective buyers. It was always, "As you of course already know, so and so." The very effort which some people make to impress us with their superior knowledge acts as a negative barrier that is hard to overcome in the process of rendering our minds "neutral." Instead of "neutralizing" our minds, such people antagonize us and make impossible the operation of the principle of suggestion in influencing us.

As a befitting climax for this lesson, I shall quote an article written by Dr. Henry R. Rose, entitled "The Mind Doctor at Work." This is the clearest elucidation on the subject of suggestion that I have ever seen, and fully substantiates all that I have discovered in my research on this subject.

This article, within itself, constitutes the finest lesson on suggestion that I have ever seen:

> **"If my wife dies, I will not believe there is a God." His wife was ill of pneumonia. This is the way he greeted me when I reached his home. She had sent for me. The doctor had told her she could not recover. She had called her husband and two sons to her bedside and bidden them goodbye. Then he asked that I, her minister, be sent for. I found the**

husband in the front room sobbing and the sons doing their best to brace him up. I went in to see his wife. She was breathing with difficulty, and the trained nurse told me she was very low. I soon found that Mrs. N had sent for me to look after her two sons after she was gone. Then I said to her, "You mustn't give up. You are not going to die. You have always been a strong and healthy woman, and I do not believe God wants you to die and leave your boys to me or anyone else."

I talked to her along this line and then read the 103rd Psalm and made a prayer in which I prepared her to get well rather than to enter eternity. I told her to put her faith in God and throw her mind and will against every thought of dying. Then I left her, saying that I would come again after the church service. This was on a Sunday morning. I called that afternoon. Her husband met me with a smile. He said that the moment I had gone, his wife called him and the boys into the room and said, "Dr. Rose says that I am going to get well, and I am."

She did get well. But what did it? Two things: suggestion on my part and confidence on her part. I came in the nick of time, and so great was her faith in me, that I was able to inspire faith in herself. It was that faith that tipped the scales and brought her through the pneumonia. No medicine can cure pneumonia. The physicians admit it. There are cases of pneumonia that nothing can cure. We all sadly agree to that. But there are times, as in this case, when the mind, if worked upon and worked in just the right way, will turn the tide. While there is life, there is hope; but hope must be supreme and do the good that hope was created to do.

Another remarkable case: A physician asked me to see Mrs. H. He said there was nothing organically wrong with her, but she just wouldn't eat. Having made up her mind that she could not retain anything on her stomach, she had quit eating and was slowly starving herself to death. I went to see her and found, first, that she had no religious belief. She had lost her faith in God. I also found that she had no confidence in her power to retain food. My first effort was to restore her faith in the Almighty and to get her to believe that He was with her and would give her power. Then I told her that she could eat anything. True, her confidence in me was great, and my statement impressed her. She began to eat from that day! She was out of her bed in three days, for the first time in weeks. She is a normal woman today. What did it? The same forces as in the preceding case—outside suggestion and inward confidence.

There are times when the mind is sick, and it makes the body sick. At such times, it needs a stronger mind to heal it by giving it direction and especially by giving it confidence in itself. This is called suggestion. It is transmitting your confidence and power to another, and with such force as to make the other believe as you wish and do as you will. It need not be hypnotism. You can get wonderful results with the patient wide awake and perfectly rational. He must believe in you, and you must know the workings of the human mind in order to meet his arguments and questionings completely and banish them utterly from his thoughts. Each one of us can be healers of this sort and, thus, help our fellow men.

It is now the duty of men and woman to read some of the best books on the force of the mind and learn what amazing and glorious things the mind can do to keep people well or to restore their health. We see the terrible things that wrong thinking does to people, even going to such lengths as to make them positively insane. Is it now high time we found out the good things that right thinking can do, and its power to cure not only mental disorders, but physical diseases as well?

I do not say that the mind can do everything. There is no reliable evidence that certain forms of real cancer have been cured by thinking or faith or any mental or religious process. If you would be cured of cancer, you must take it at the very beginning and treat it surgically. There is no other way, and I would feel myself a criminal if I led any reader to neglect the first symptoms of this awful malady by thinking to overcome them by mental suggestion. But the mind can do so much with so many, many types of human indisposition and disease that we ought to rely upon it more than we do.

Napoleon during his campaign in Egypt went among his soldiers who were dying by the hundreds of the black plague. He touched one of them and lifted a second, to inspire the others not to be afraid, for the awful disease seemed to be spread as much by the imagination as in any other way. Goethe tells us that he himself went where there was malignant fever and never contracted it because he put forth his will. These giants among men knew something we are slowly beginning to find out—the power of auto-suggestion. This means the influence we have upon ourselves by believing we cannot catch a disease or be sick. There is something about the operation of the automatic mind by which it rises above disease germs and bids defiance to them when we resolve not to let the thought of them frighten us or when we go in and out among the sick, even the contagiously sick, without thinking anything about it.

Imagination . . . certainly will kill a man. There are authentic cases on record of men having actually died because they imagined they were cut with a knife across the jugular vein, when in reality, a piece of ice was used and water was allowed to drop so that they could hear it and imagine their blood was running out. They had been blindfolded before the experiment was begun. No matter how well you may be when you start for work in the morning, if everybody you meet should say to you, "How ill you look," it will not be long before you begin to feel ill, and if that thing keeps up all day, you will arrive home at night as limp as a rag and ready for a doctor. Such is the fatal power of imagination or auto-suggestion.

The first thing, then, is to remember what pranks your imagination can play upon you, and be on your guard. Do not allow yourself to think that awful things are the matter with you or are going to be the matter with you. If you do, you will suffer.

Young medical students not infrequently think they have every disease they hear discussed or analyzed in the classroom. Some of them have imaginations so vivid that they actually come down with the disease. Yes, an imagined disease is perfectly possible and may be just as painful as a disease gotten in some other way. An imaginary pain is just as painful as any other kind of pain. No medicine can cure it. It must be removed by imagining it away.

Dr. Schofield describes the case of a woman who had a tumor. They put her on the operating table and gave her anesthetics. Lo and behold, the tumor immediately disappeared. No operation was necessary. But when she came back to consciousness, the tumor returned! The physician then learned that she had been living with a relative who had a real tumor, and her imagination was so great that she had imagined this one upon herself. She was put on the operating table again, given anesthetics, and then she was strapped around the middle so that the tumor could not artificially return. When she revived, she was told that a successful operation had been performed, but that it would be necessary to wear the bandage for several days. She believed the doctor, and when the bandage was finally removed, the tumor did not return. No operation whatever had been performed. He had simply relieved her subconscious mind, and the imagination had nothing to work upon save the idea of health, and as she had never been really sick, of course she became normal.

If what you think and brood upon can go so far as to produce an imitation tumor, do you not see how careful you should be never to imagine you have a disease of any kind?

The very best way to cure your imagination is at night, just as you go to bed. In the night season, the automatic (subconscious) mind has everything its own way, and the thoughts you give it before your day's mind (conscious mind) goes to sleep will go on working it all through the night. This may seem a foolish statement, but prove it a true one by the following test. You want to get up at seven o'clock in the morning or, say, some other hour than your regular one for rising. Now say to yourself on going to bed, "I must rise at seven o'clock." Turn that thought over to your automatic mind with absolute confidence, and you will waken at seven o'clock. This thing is done over and over again, and it is done because the subconscious self is awake all night, and when seven o'clock comes, it taps you on the shoulder, so to speak, and wakes you up. But you must trust it. If you have the least doubt that you will not wake up, it is likely to interfere with the whole process. Faith in your automatic mechanism causes it to operate just as you direct it before you fall asleep.

Here is a great secret, and it will help you overcome many a fault and deplorable habit. Tell yourself that you are through worrying, through drinking, through stammering, or whatever else you wish to quit, and then leave the job to the subconscious mind at night. Do this night after night, and mark, you will win.

∽

Summary

You have learned from this lesson that suggestion is the principle through which we may influence the minds and actions of others. We have learned that the mind will attract to it the object upon which it dwells most extensively. We have learned that the mind must be "neutralized" before it can be influenced by suggestion, and we have learned that before the mind can be "neutralized," a state of credulousness greater than normal must exist.

We have learned that hypnotism is nothing more than suggestion operating through a mind that has been "neutralized."

We have learned that suggestion will actually destroy body cells and develop disease, and that it will also restore body cells and destroy disease germs.

We have learned that through the principle of suggestion, we can cause a large percentage of an audience to smell peppermint when, in reality, no such odor is within smelling distance.

We have learned that confidence must be created in a person's mind before one can "neutralize" that mind. We have learned that human sympathy is a strong factor through which to build confidence, and that we can readily "neutralize" the mind of the person for whom we express full sympathy or love.

We have learned that more desirable results can be obtained (through suggestion) by complimenting a workman and causing him to think well of himself than is possible through reprimand.

We have learned the tremendous advantage of placing our ideas and thoughts in the minds of others in such a way as to make them feel that they are the originators.

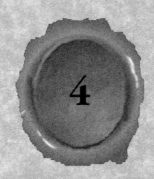

The Law of
Retaliation

*T*his lesson brings us to a discussion of one of the most important major principles of psychology, the law of retaliation, as follows:

The human mind resembles mother earth in that it will reproduce, in kind, that which is planted in it through the five physical senses. The preponderance of tendency upon the part of the mind is to "retaliate in kind," reciprocating all acts of kindness and resenting all acts of injustice and unkindness. Whether acting through the principle of suggestion or auto-suggestion, the mind directs muscular action that harmonizes with the sensory impressions it receives; therefore, if you would have me "retaliate in kind," you can do so by placing in my mind the sensory impressions or suggestions out of which you wish me to create the necessary appropriate muscular action. Injure or displease me, and like a flash, my mind will direct appropriate muscular action, "retaliating in kind."

In studying the law of retaliation, we are carried, to an extent, into what we might call the field of unknown mental phenomena—the field of physics. The phenomena discovered in this great field have not been reduced to a science, but again, let us bear in mind the fact that this shall not hinder us from making practical use of certain principles which we have discovered in this field, even though we cannot trace these principles back to first cause. One of these principles is that which we have stated above as our fourth general principle of psychology, namely, "like attracts like."

No scientist has ever satisfactorily explained this principle, but the fact still remains that it is a known principle; therefore, just as we make intelligent use of electricity without knowing what it is, let us also make intelligent use of the principles of retaliation.

It is an encouraging sign to see that modern writers are giving their attention more and more to the study of the law of retaliation. Some of them call it one thing, and some call it another, but all of them seem to agree on the chief fundamental of the principle as follows: "Like attracts like!"

The latest writer to turn her attention to this subject is Mrs. Woodrow Wilson. Her article follows:

> **"There seems to be a mental law to the effect that whatever generally occupies the mind is almost certain to take form in the objective. Each of us proves that in his own experience dozens of times.**
>
> **"For instance, you may come across a word you are not familiar with. To the best of your knowledge, you have never heard it nor seen it before, and yet after your discovery of it, you will encounter it again and again.**
>
> **"This fact has recently come to me in an odd sort of a way. I have been doing a great deal of reading and research on a subject which has interested me and, yet, which would certainly never be classed as live news matter. I do not remember ever having seen it mentioned in any current publication, but since I have been familiarizing myself with it, I have clipped a large number of articles treating of one phase or another of it from various magazines and newspapers.**
>
> **"You can easily follow the workings of this law, whatever it is, down to the smallest details.**
>
> **"A friend came to see me a day or two ago and stood transfixed upon the threshold of my sitting room.**
>
> **" 'Flowers!' she exclaimed. 'Roses?'**

"There was such horror in her tones that I thought she was reproving me for buying anything but thrift stamps. She explained, however, that she was suffering from rose cold, which afflicts those who are subject to it at the same time each year, just as hay fever does.

" 'It comes in June,' she said, 'when the roses are blooming, and even a whiff of their fragrance will set me sneezing for twenty minutes.'

" 'It's rather a rare disease, isn't it?' I asked after I had whisked my flowers out of sight.

" 'Not at all,' she replied. 'Very common. Every other person I meet has it.'

"Now, I meet just as many people as she does during the day, perhaps more, and yet with the exception of herself, I know no one who suffers from this malady.

"Again, why is it that, if we find our thoughts turning persistently to some particular person, we are very apt to hear from him or meet him within a short time? We may not have given him a thought for months or years, and yet 'behold his shadow on the floor.'

"I know there are various explanations for these phenomena, but none of them is entirely satisfactory. The effect, however, is as if we, unconsciously to ourselves, sent out wireless messages into the universe and received the responses. Like seeks like.

"May not this account for the fact that people with grievances are always well supplied with material for fresh ones, that the mournful people have plenty to mourn about, that the most dreadful of pests, the man or woman with a chip on their shoulder, invariably arouses a burning desire in the breast of the meek and innocent bystander to knock it off?

"We all know people who are just naturally lucky.

"Everything seems to come their way. They don't have to climb trees and laboriously pick the fruit off the branches. They merely stretch out a hand, and the plums fall into it.

"I heard a woman complaining of the inequalities of fate recently and comparing her lot with that of an acquaintance.

"'Just look at her,' she said. 'Here I have worked and worried and schemed and contrived for years. Anything that I get comes by the hardest kind of effort and usually after a thousand disappointments. But she, while not half so clever as I, nor so diligent a worker, is yet a sort of a magnet attracting to herself the good things which fly past me. There's no such thing as justice.'

"But she affirmed the justice of the law even while she denied it. I know the lucky woman as well as I knew the unlucky one. The difference between the two was that one was always expecting the worst and preparing for it, and the other looked forward to agreeable and pleasant things. She took them as a matter of course and made them welcome. It was always the top o' the morning to her.

"There are days which are well known to all of us when everything goes wrong. There is certainly no malign power that is trying to thwart us and make

**us miserable, although it is often easier to believe so
than to understand why one disturbing
circumstance should follow another from early
morn to dewy."**

One does not have to be a master of psychology to accept the truth
of Mrs. Woodrow Wilson's article—it is a truth which we have all
experienced, yet it is a truth to which most of us have attached little or
no significance.

It is in no spirit of irreverence that I place prayer, that mighty
worker of miracles, in the great field of unknown phenomena. I am a
firm believer in prayer! It has worked wonders for me, yet I know
nothing whatsoever as to the first cause to which we appeal through
prayer. I know this, however: that through consistent, persistent
effort, prayer will break down all obstacles and force the seemingly
unfathomable problems to give up their secrets!

For four years, I prayed persistently for the truth that was wrapped
up in what appeared to be an impenetrable secret in another's heart.
The information I wanted was known to only one other person. The
very nature of the information almost necessitated its being held
inviolable forever. At about the end of the fourth year, I carried my
prayers a step further than I had ever done before—I determined that
I would shut my eyes and behold a picture of the exact information
that I wanted. Strange as it may seem, I had hardly closed my eyes
before the outlines of the picture began to trace themselves in my
consciousness, and within two or three minutes, I had my answer!

It seemed so strange to me that, at first, I believed what I had seen
was nothing but a hallucination, but I did not have to wait long before
I knew better. The next day, I met the person in whose heart the
secret was locked, and I was told by that person that for four years
some strange force had been tugging at her heart strings, trying to
induce her to tell me a story which she said she now wished to relate.
In that story was the information that I wanted and for which I had
prayed for four years!

Some would tell us that Divine Power produced this remarkable result, while others would be inclined to explain it through mental telepathy. My own opinion is that every thought vibration on the subject which was produced in my mind, at the time of prayer, was registered in the subconscious mind of the other person, having traveled through the ethereal air currents just as vibrations sent by a wireless outfit traveled from one instrument to another, and that these thought vibrations finally caused the alchemic change to take place in her mind which resulted in her decision to give me the information I wanted. Mind you, I said that I believe this is what took place—as to the original cause which made possible the transmission of thought through the open air, I venture no suggestions!

On another occasion, which is an extreme in the other direction, I accomplished a remarkable result through prayer in less than a minute and a half. An important business transaction was under way, I had made an offer, and it had been turned down coldly. The person to whom the offer was made stepped out of his office for not longer than a minute and a half. While he was gone, I sent out a message through what we call prayer, in which I asked for a reversal of his ultimatum. He came back in and announced, without my saying a word, that he had changed his mind and would accept my offer.

Before getting away from the subject of "unknown phenomena," permit me to once more remind you that this course of scientific instruction has no connection whatsoever with any religious faith, and whenever we refer, directly or indirectly, to any subject connected with religion, we do so for purpose of comparison only.

Millions of people have found happiness and contentment through the great unknown phenomenon which we call prayer. I have no desire to cause anyone to change his or her belief in prayer. To the contrary, I would do all possible to strengthen that belief!

Neither have I any intention whatsoever of reducing prayer to a purely scientific phenomenon. Whether our prayers produce such wonderful results, as we know they do, through the principle of auto-suggestion or through the influence of outside Divine forces over which we have no control is of but little importance. We are apt to pray with more *faith* and *persistence* by directing our prayers to the Divine source, and this, within itself, would warrant our refraining from adopting the scientific principle of auto-suggestion as an explanation of the great phenomenon of prayer.

Late one afternoon, I was sitting at my desk waiting for Mrs. Hill to join me. The office force had gone, and I was the only person in the room. I leaned over and rested my face on my hands, covering my eyes with the ends of my fingers. Mind you, I was not asleep, for I had not been in that position more than thirty seconds. Then a strange thing happened. It was almost time for Mrs. Hill to arrive. I heard her scream! I saw her knocked down by an automobile. I saw a policeman lift her up from the pavement and place her on the sidewalk. I saw the blood on her face.

I opened my eyes and looked around. I could not have been dreaming because I was not asleep. Soon I heard Mrs. Hill's footsteps. She was excited and almost out of breath. Sure enough, she had been almost run down by an automobile at the very spot where I saw her. She did scream, and the policeman did pull her back on the sidewalk, just as I had seen him do. And, as near as we could estimate, all of this happened at the very moment when I saw it, sitting at my desk with my eyes closed, a block away from the actual scene!

In the state of Illinois, near the city of Chicago, a few years ago, a farmer left his home one morning and started toward his fields to work. He had gone but a short distance when he experienced a strange feeling that impelled him to arbitrarily return to the house. He paid no attention to it at first, but it became stronger and more insistent. Finally, he could go no further, so he turned and started toward the house. The nearer he got, the faster he wanted to walk until he finally started to run. When he got inside the house, he found his daughter lying on the floor with her throat cut. Her assailant had gone but a few seconds before his arrival.

What caused these strange phenomena, we do not know, unless it was mental telepathy. These two cases are cited because both of them are authentic. I could cite more than a dozen similar cases which would have a strong tendency to prove the existence of mental telepathy through which thoughts actually pass from one mind to another just as the vibration passes from one instrument to another through wireless telegraphy. Of course these minds must be harmoniously attuned to each other, just as the wireless instruments must be properly attuned, or the thoughts will not register.

These examples of what we might term unknown phenomena are mentioned in connection with this lesson for the reason that we want you to stop and consider what the possibilities are for making practical use of the law of retaliation, which operates directly through the five physical senses. We do not have to depend upon unknown phenomena or mental telepathy, which are but slightly understood at this time; we can reach and influence the human mind directly through the law of retaliation and the principle of suggestion. Suggestion is the medium through which we reach the mind of another, and the law of retaliation is the principle through which we plant in that mind the seed that we wish to see take root and grow.

You know what *retaliate* means!

In the sense that we are using it here, it means to "return like for like," and not merely to avenge or to seek revenge, as is commonly meant by the use of this word.

If I do you an injury, you retaliate at first opportunity. If I say unjust things about you, you will retaliate in kind, even in greater measure!

On the other hand, if I do you a favor, you will reciprocate even in greater measure if possible.

Thus, we are following the impulse of our nature, through the "law of retaliation"!

Through the proper use of this law, I can get you to do whatever I wish you to do. If I wish you to dislike me and to lend your influence toward damaging me, I can accomplish this result by inflicting upon you the sort of treatment that I want you to inflict upon me through retaliation.

If I wish your respect, your friendship, and your cooperation, I can get these by extending to you my friendship and cooperation.

On these statements, I know that we are together. You can compare these statements with your own experience, and you will see how beautifully they harmonize.

How often have you heard the remark, "What a wonderful personality that person has." How often have you met people whose personalities you coveted?

The man who attracts you to him through his pleasing personality is merely making use of the law of harmonious attraction or the law of retaliation, both of which, when analyzed, mean that "like attracts like."

If you will study, understand, and make intelligent use of the law of retaliation, you will be an efficient and successful salesman. When you have mastered this simple law and learned how to use it, you will have learned all that can be learned about salesmanship.

The first, and probably the most important, step to be taken in mastering this law is to cultivate complete self-control. You must learn to take all sorts of punishment and abuse without retaliating in kind. This self-control is a part of the price you must pay for mastery of the law of retaliation.

When an angry person starts in to vilify and abuse you, justly or unjustly, just remember that if you retaliate in a like manner, you are being drawn down to that person's mental level; therefore, that person is dominating you!

On the other hand, if you refuse to become angry, if you retain your self-composure and remain calm and serene, you retain all your ordinary faculties through which to reason. You take the other fellow by surprise. You retaliate with a weapon with the use of which he is unfamiliar; consequently, you easily dominate him.

Like attracts like! There's no denying this!

Literally speaking, every person with whom you come in contact is a mental looking glass in which you may see a perfect reflection of your own mental attitude.

As an example of direct application of the law of retaliation, let us cite an experience that I recently had with my two small boys, Napoleon Junior and James.

We were on our way to the park to feed the birds and squirrels. Napoleon Junior had bought a bag of peanuts, and James had bought a box of Crackerjack. James took a notion to sample the peanuts. Without asking permission, he reached over and made a grab for the bag. He missed, and Napoleon Junior "retaliated" with his left fist, which landed rather briskly on James' jaw.

I said to James, "Now, see here, son, you didn't go about getting those peanuts in the right manner. Let me show you how to get them." It all happened so quickly that I hadn't the slightest idea when I spoke what I was going to suggest to James, but I sparred for time to analyze the occurrence and work out a better way, if possible, than that adopted by him.

Then I thought of the experiments we had been making in connection with the law of retaliation, so I said to James, "Open your box of Crackerjack and offer your little brother some and see what happens." After considerable coaxing, I persuaded him to do this. Then a remarkable thing happened—a happening out of which I learned my greatest lesson in salesmanship! Before Napoleon Junior would touch the Crackerjack, he insisted on pouring some of his peanuts into James' overcoat pocket. He "retaliated in kind"! Out of this simple experiment with two small boys, I learned more about the art of managing them than I could have learned in any other manner. Incidentally, my boys are beginning to learn how to manipulate this law of retaliation, which saves them many a physical combat.

None of us have advanced far beyond Napoleon Junior and James as far as the operation and influence of the law of retaliation is concerned. We are all just grown-up children and easily influenced through this principle. The habit of "retaliating in kind" is so universally practiced among us that we can properly call this habit the law of retaliation. If a person presents us with a gift, we never feel satisfied until we have "retaliated" with something as good as or better than that which we received. If a person speaks well of us, we increase our admiration for that person, and we "retaliate" in return!

Through the principle of retaliation, we can actually convert our enemies into loyal friends. If you have an enemy whom you wish to convert into a friend, you can prove the truth of this statement if you will forget that dangerous millstone hanging around your neck which we call "pride" (stubbornness). Make a habit of speaking to this enemy with unusual cordiality. Go out of your way to favor him in every manner possible. He may seem immovable at first, but gradually, he will give way to your influence and "retaliate in kind"! The hottest coals of fire ever heaped upon the head of one who has wronged you are the coals of human kindness.

> **"One morning in August, 1863, a young clergyman was called out of bed in a hotel at Lawrence, Kansas. The man who called him was one of Quantrell's guerrillas, and he wanted him to hurry downstairs and be shot. All over the border that morning, people were being murdered. A band of raiders had ridden in early to perpetrate the Lawrence massacre.**
>
> **"The guerrilla who called the clergyman was impatient. The latter, when fully awake, was horrified by what he saw going on through his window. As he came downstairs, the guerrilla demanded his watch and money and then wanted to know if he was an abolitionist. The clergyman was trembling. But he decided that if he was to die then and there, it would not be with a lie on his lips. So he said that he was, and followed up the admission with a remark that immediately turned the whole affair into another channel.**

"He and the guerrilla sat down on the porch, while people were being killed through the town, and had a long talk. It lasted until the raiders were ready to leave. When the clergyman's guerrilla mounted to join his confederates, he was strictly on the defensive. He handed back the New Englander's valuables, apologized for disturbing him, and asked to be thought well of.

"That clergyman lived many years after the Lawrence massacre. What did he say to the guerrilla? What was there in his personality that led the latter to sit down and talk? What did they talk about?

"'Are you a Yankee abolitionist?' the guerrilla had asked. 'Yes, I am,' was the reply, 'and you know very well that you ought to be ashamed of what you're doing.'

"This drew the matter directly to a moral issue. It brought the guerrilla up roundly. The clergyman was only a stripling beside this seasoned border ruffian. But he threw a burden of moral proof onto the raider, and in a moment, the latter was trying to demonstrate that he might be a better fellow than circumstances would seem to indicate.

"After waking this New Englander to kill him on account of his politics, he spent twenty minutes on the witness stand trying to prove an alibi. He went into his personal history at length. He explained matters from the time when he had been a tough little kid who wouldn't say his prayers, and became quite sentimental in recalling how one thing had led to another, and that to something worse, until— well, here he was, and 'a might bad business to be in,

pardner.' His last request in riding away was, 'Now, pardner, don't think too hard of me, will you?'"

From *The Lawrence Massacre by a Band of Missouri Ruffians Under Quantrell*, by J. S. Boughton and Richard Cordley

The New England clergyman made use of the law of retaliation, whether he knew it at that time or not. Imagine what would have happened had he come downstairs with a revolver in his hand and started to meet physical force with physical force!

But he didn't do this! He mastered the guerrilla because he fought him with a force that was unknown to the brigand.

Why is it that when once a man begins to make money, the whole world seems to beat a pathway to his door?

Take any person that you know who enjoys financial success, and he will tell you that he is being constantly sought, and that opportunities to make money are constantly being urged upon him!

"To him that hath shall be given, but to him that hath not shall be taken away even that which he hath" (Matthew 25:29).

This quotation from the Bible used to seem ridiculous to me, yet how true it is when reduced to its concrete meaning.

Yes, *"to him that hath shall be given"!* If he "hath" failure, lack of self-confidence, hatred, or lack of self-control, to him shall these qualities be given in still greater abundance! But, if he "hath" success, self-confidence, self-control, patience, and persistence, to him shall these qualities be increased!

Sometimes it may be necessary to meet force with force until we overpower our opponent or adversary, but while he is down is a splendid time to complete the "retaliation" by taking him by the hand and showing him a better way to settle disputes.

Like attracts like! Germany sought to bathe her sword in human blood, in ruthless escapade of conquest. As a result, she has drawn the "retaliation in kind" of most of the civilized world.

It is for you to decide what you want your fellowmen to do, and it is for you to get them to do it through the law of retaliation!

"The Divine economy is automatic and very simple: we receive only that which we give."

How true it is that "we receive only that which we give"! It is not that which we *wish for* that comes back to us, but that which we *give*.

I implore you to make use of this law, not alone for material gain, but, better still, for the attainment of happiness and good will toward men.

This, after all, is the only real success for which to strive.

Summary

In this lesson, we have learned a great principle—probably the most important major principle of psychology! We have learned that our thoughts and actions toward others resemble an electric magnet which attracts to us the same sort of thought and the same sort of action that we, ourselves, create.

We have learned that "like attracts like," whether in thought or in expression of thought through bodily action. We have learned that the human mind responds in kind to whatever thought impressions it receives. We have learned that the human mind resembles mother earth in that it will reproduce a crop of muscular action which corresponds, in kind, to the sensory impressions planted in it. We have learned that kindness begets kindness, and unkindness and injustice beget unkindness and injustice.

We have learned that our actions toward others, whether of kindness or unkindness, justice or injustice, come back to us in even larger measure! We have learned that the human mind responds in kind to all sensory impressions it receives; therefore, we know what we must do to influence any desired action upon the part of another. We have learned that "pride" and "stubbornness" must be brushed away before we can make use of the law of retaliation in a constructive way. We have not learned what the law of retaliation is, but we have

learned how it works and what it will do; therefore, it only
us to make intelligent use of this great principle.

Pills for Pessimists
J. W. Wigelsworth, D.N.

The devil worry spoils more digestions than whiskey.

Fussing, fuming, fearing, and apprehending what?

Usually nothing.

They are all pure and simple evidences of ignorance or bodily
distortion.

Your body is influenced by your mind.

Your mind is influenced by your body.

An untrained mind worries.

A sick body stimulates worry.

A worrier's thoughts run riot.

They roll in, one crowding the other out of order and arrangement.

It's uncontrolled thinking.

Worriers are like ships on the angry ocean, tossed here and there
without any self-control.

The worrier is either physically disorganized, or he proves his lack
of confidence in God by worrying.

Worry is cowardice if your body is all right.

And besides, "I am an old man and have worried much over things
that never happened."

Fear freezes us up and puts our functions into cold storage.

You stop when you fear.

You chill your vitals and stand like a frozen being.

What is fear? Just, "I'm afraid":

You must face the music of life.

Your future is not today, but today makes your future.

Fretting and fearing make a fitting future for themselves.

If you want to be sick—want to devitalize and destroy your
body—then fear and worry about things.

It's a sure method of making a diseased future. *Let this soak in.*

Hate is ungodly and ruins our bodies and minds.

Beauty is "skin deep," they say.

"Skin deep" beauty becomes "skin deep," body full, disposition ruining ugliness under the magic wand of hate.

Hate is a low-down, degrading, uncivilized, detestable thing.

The woman in the gutter, in the lowest walks of life—is a queen beside the hater.

You can't be good.

You can't be reasonable.

You can't think.

You can't eat.

Hate and your body will show its mark—so will your future.

You can't do good.

You can't be sane—and be jealous.

You should consider your mind sacred. If you desecrate it with jealousy, you are ugly, unstable mentally, and an undesirable member of society.

These four—Worry, Fear, Hate, and Jealousy—are the ravages of good health.

Your body and mind must both be right to be healthy.

An unhealthy body makes an unhealthy mind.

An unhealthy mind makes an unhealthy body.

A real doctor must take these things into consideration.

Good thoughts lead to health, wealth, and happiness.

Bad thoughts lead to sickness, poverty, and hell.

Look into the mirror and smile at yourself.

5

The Power of
Your Mind

The human mind is a composite of many qualities and tendencies. It consists of likes and dislikes, optimism and pessimism, hatred and love, constructiveness and destructiveness, kindness and cruelty. The mind is made up of all these qualities and more. It is a blending of them all, some minds showing one of these qualities dominating and other minds showing others dominating.

❧

Learn How to Use That Wonderful Mind of Yours

The dominating qualities are largely determined by one's environment, training, and associates, and particularly by one's own thoughts! Any thought held constantly in the mind, or any thought dwelt upon through concentration and brought into the conscious mind often, attracts to it those qualities of the human mind which it most resembles.

A thought is like a seed planted in the ground in that it brings back a crop after its kind, multiplies, and grows; therefore, it is dangerous to allow the mind to hold any thought which is destructive. Such thoughts must sooner or later seek release through physical action.

Through the principle of auto-suggestion—that is, thoughts held in the mind and concentrated upon—any thought will soon begin to crystallize into action.

If the principle of auto-suggestion were generally understood and taught in the public schools, it would change the whole moral and economic standards of the world inside of twenty years. Through this principle, the human mind can rid itself of its destructive tendencies by constantly dwelling upon its constructive tendencies. The qualities of the human mind need the sunlight of nourishment and use to keep

them alive. Throughout the universe, there is a law of nourishment and use which applies to everything that lives and grows. This law has decreed that every living thing which is neither nourished nor used must die, and this applies to the qualities of the human mind which we have mentioned.

The only way to develop any quality of the mind is to concentrate upon it, think about it, and use it. Evil tendencies of the mind can be blotted out by starving them to death through disuse!

What would it be worth to the young, plastic mind of the child to understand this principle and commence to make use of it early in life, beginning with kindergarten?

The principle of auto-suggestion is one of the fundamental major laws of applied psychology. Through a proper understanding of this principle and with the cooperation of the writers, philosophers, schoolteachers, and preachers, the whole tendency of the human mind can be directed toward constructive effort inside of twenty years or less.

What are you going to do about it?

May it not be a good plan, as far as you are concerned individually, to wait for someone to start a movement for general education along this line, but commence now to make use of this principle for the benefit of you and yours?

Your children may not be fortunate enough to receive this training in school, but there is nothing to hinder you from giving it to them in your home.

You may have been unfortunate in that you never had an opportunity to study and understand the principle of auto-suggestion when you were going to school, but there is nothing to hinder you from studying, understanding, and applying to your own efforts this principle from now on.

Learn something about that wonderful machine which we call the human mind. It is your real source of power. If you are ever to free yourself of petty worries and financial want, it will be through the efforts of that wonderful mind of yours.

Your editor is still a young man, yet he has positive evidence in many thousands of cases of the transformation of both men and women from failure to success in remarkably short periods of time, ranging all the way from a few hours to a few months.

The magazine you hold in your hands is concrete evidence of the soundness of the argument that the individual can control his economic destiny, because it is a success which was built out of fifteen years of failure!

You can turn your past failure into success if you will understand and intelligently apply the principles of applied psychology. You can get to wherever you wish to go in life. You can find happiness instantly, once you master this principle, and you can build financial success as rapidly as you comply with the established practices and principles of economics.

There is nothing that savors of occultism in the human mind. It functions in harmony with the physical and economic laws and principles. You do not need the assistance of any person on earth in the manipulation of your own mind so it will function as you want it to. Your mind is something which you control, no matter what your station in life may be, provided always that you exercise the right instead of permitting others to do so for you.

Learn something of the powers of your mind. It will free you of the curse of fear and fill you with inspiration and courage.

❧

How to Attract People to You Through the Law of Retaliation

To achieve fame or accumulate a big fortune requires the cooperation of your fellowmen. Whatever position one holds and whatever fortune one acquires must, to be permanent, be by sufferance of one's fellowmen.

You could no more remain in a position of honor without the good will of the neighborhood than you could fly to the moon, and as for holding a big fortune without the consent of your fellowmen, it would

be impossible, not only to hold it, but to acquire it in the first place, except by inheritance.

The peaceful enjoyment of money or position surely depends upon the extent to which you attract people to you. It does not require the farsighted philosopher to see that a man who enjoys the good will of all with whom he comes in contact can have anything within the gift of the people with whom he associates.

The roadway, then, to fame and fortune, or either, leads straight through the hearts of one's fellowmen.

There may be other ways of gaining the good will of one's fellowmen except through the operation of the law of retaliation, but if there is, this writer has never discovered it.

THIS!!!

Through the law of retaliation, you can induce people to send back to you that which you give to them. There is no guesswork about this—no element of chance—no uncertainty.

Let us see just how to go about harnessing this law so it will work for us instead of against us. To begin with, we need not tell you that the tendency of the human heart is to strike back, returning stroke for stroke every effort, whether of cooperation or of antagonism.

true!!

Antagonize a person and, as surely as two and two are four, that person will retaliate in kind. Befriend a person or confer upon him some act of kindness, and he will also reciprocate in kind.

Never mind the person who does not respond in accordance with this principle. He is merely the proverbial exception. By the law of averages, the great majority of people will quite unconsciously respond.

The man who goes about with a chip on his shoulder finds a dozen people a day who take delight in knocking it off, a fact to which you can easily subscribe if you have ever tried going about with a chip on your shoulder. You need no proof that the man who carries a smile on his face and who always has a word of kindness for everyone he meets is universally liked, while the opposite type is just as generally disliked.

This law of retaliation is a powerful force which touches the whole universe, constantly attracting and repelling. You will find it in the heart of the acorn which falls to the ground and, in response to the warmth of the sunlight, bursts forth into a tiny sprig consisting of two small leaves which finally grow and attracts to itself the necessary elements to constitute a sturdy oak tree.

No one ever heard of an acorn attracting to it anything except the cells out of which an oak tree grows. No one ever saw a tree which was half oak and half poplar. The center of the acorn forms affinities only with those elements which constitute an oak tree.

Every thought which finds abode in the human brain attracts elements after its kind, whether of destruction or construction, kindness or unkindness. You can no more concentrate your mind on hatred and dislike and expect a crop of the opposite brand than you could expect an acorn to develop into a poplar tree. It simply is not in harmony with the law of retaliation.

Throughout the universe, everything in the form of matter gravitates to certain centers of attraction. People of similar intellect and tendencies are attracted to each other. The human mind forms affinities only with other minds which are harmonious and have similar tendencies; therefore, the class of person which you attract to you will depend upon the tendencies of your own mind. You control those tendencies and can direct them along any line you choose, attracting to you any sort of person you wish.

This is a law of nature. It is an immutable law, and it works whether we make conscious use of it or not.

❧

How Great Fortunes Are Made

Mr. Carnegie has passed away, leaving a fortune of several hundred millions of dollars after having given away many millions.

Thousands of people there are who envied Carnegie his millions. Many more thousands there are who have puzzled their brains trying to think out some plan or scheme through which they could build up a fortune such as the one which Carnegie possessed.

Let us tell you how Carnegie built his fortune. Maybe it will give you an idea that will help you in building yours. In the first place, it is well to remember that Carnegie was not possessed of more ability than the average man enjoys. He was not a genius, and he did nothing which almost any other man could not duplicate.

Mr. Carnegie accumulated his millions by selecting, combining, and managing other men's brains. He realized early in life that any undertaking such as the steel business required more talent than any one man possessed. He also realized that most industries and businesses require at least two types of men—one the caretaker and the other the promoter. Carnegie selected the men he wanted, organized them, directed them, and kept them enthusiastic and eager to render the greatest amount of service. He got them to cooperate with one another and with him.

No man can build a fortune such as that which Carnegie controlled without the use of other men's brains. The amount which a single brain can produce, accumulate, and own, acting independently of other brains, is comparatively little, but the amount which one brain can accumulate and control when acting in harmony with other highly organized minds is practically unlimited.

If you want to become wealthy, learn how to attract to you men and women who have that which you do not possess in the way of brain capacity. If you are of the promoter type, select your associates so that some of them at least will be of the caretaker type. A well-rounded-out partnership or organization of men, to be successful, must be made up of men who possess all the requisite qualities essential for success. Some men can acquire but cannot conserve assets. Other men can conserve but cannot acquire. The two types, working in harmony, can both acquire and conserve.

Many a business has grown sickly and finally passed into bankruptcy for no reason other than the fact that it was managed by men who had too much of one sort of talent and too little or none at all of other necessary sorts. Business requires something more than capital with which to succeed. It requires well-balanced brains, made up of the various shades and blendings of the caretaker and the promoter type. }

◦◦◦

The Greatest Age in History

This is no time for the person who believes only that which he understands. Neither is it a favorable time for the person who doubts the ability of the human mind to look behind the curtain of time down the ages and there see the handwriting of nature.

Nature is yielding up her secrets to all who wish to see. She no longer uses the lightning in the clouds to scare ignorant, superstitious humanity. That force has now been harnessed. It pulls our trains, cooks our meals, drives our wheels of industry, and carries the whisper of our voices around the earth in the fractional part of a second.

Electricity is exactly the same force now that it was three hundred years ago, yet we knew nothing about it then except that we believed it was only destructive! We did not know that it would one day serve as man's greatest servant, obediently carrying out his commands. We did not understand electricity; therefore, we made no attempt to master it until recent years. We know comparatively nothing about electricity now, but we have commenced to experiment with it, and that is a step toward discovery of what it is and what it will do when we learn more about it.

Electricity now carries the human voice around the earth. One day, it will carry the human body to any given point with speed heretofore undreamed of. Our method of harnessing electricity is now very crude. We shall learn how to manipulate, regulate, and control this universal energy through a process as simple as that through which we now draw water out of a spigot, through the aid of gravity.

How can we discover the possibilities of electricity?

How can we tap this great reservoir of energy and use it at will?

We can do this only through experimentation—through the use of imagination! This is decidedly the age of imagination, inquiry, and experiment. The human race has begun to throw off the shackles of fear and doubt and take hold of the tools of progress which have been lying at our feet throughout the ages.

The present is the most wonderful age in the period of history of the human race—wonderful not only in its mechanical development, but also in its mental development. We have not only discovered how to fly in the air, swim under the ocean, and talk around the earth, but we have discovered the cause of all this achievement—the human mind!

The last fifty years have been the most active period in the world's history as far as discovery through science is concerned. The next fifty years probably will take us as far into the development of the human mind as the past fifty years have taken us into the mastery of physics and mere mechanical devices.

❧

Quit Quarreling with Your Fellowmen

The time and energy which we spend in striking back at those who anger us would make us independently wealthy if this great force were directed toward constructive effort—to building instead of tearing down!

It is the belief of this writer that the average person spends three-fourths of his or her lifetime in useless, destructive effort.

There is but one real way to punish a person who has wronged you, and that is by returning good for evil. The hottest coals ever heaped upon a human being's head are acts of kindness in return for acts of cruelty.

Time spent in hatred not only is wasted, but it smothers the only worthwhile emotions of the human heart, and renders a person useless for constructive work. Thoughts of hatred do not harm anyone except the person who indulges in them.

Whiskey and morphine are no more deleterious to the human body than are thoughts of hatred and anger. Lucky is the person who has grown to be big enough and wise enough to rise above intolerance, selfishness, greed, and petty jealousies. These are the things which blot out the better impulses of the human soul and open the human heart to violence.

If anger ever profited a man anything, this writer never heard of it. Great souls are usually housed in human beings who are slow at anger and who seldom try to destroy one of their fellowmen or defeat him in his undertakings.

The man or woman who can forgive and truly forget an injury by a fellow man is to be envied. Such souls rise to heights of happiness which most mortals never enjoy.

How long, oh God, how long will it be until the human race will learn to walk down the pathway of life, arm in arm, helping one another in a spirit of love, instead of trying to cut one another down? How long will it be until we learn that the only real success in life is measured by the extent to which we serve humanity? How long will it be until we learn that life's richest blessings are bestowed upon the person who scorns to stoop to the vulgar attempt to destroy his fellow man?

I know that this plainness of speech makes them hate me; and what is this hatred but a proof that I am speaking the truth?——this is the occasion and reason of their slander of me, and you will find out in this or in any future inquiry.

—SOCRATES

6

How to Build Self-Confidence

$\mathcal{T}$he scientific principles outlined in this lesson have brought success and happiness to millions of people. This particular treatise on "How to Build Self-Confidence" was written more than seven years ago as a part of a general course in applied psychology.

Later it was published in booklet form, and more than three hundred thousand of the booklets have been distributed. One large industrial concern presented a copy of it to every employee on its payrolls, several thousand people.

The lesson which you are about to read has an interesting history. I have evidence of more than a hundred cases of men and women finding their proper bearings in life through the aid of that which you are about to read.

> An attractive personality is something that is always found near a heart that beats with kindness and sympathy for struggling humanity.

The most striking example of immediate transformation of failure into success, through the aid of this article, happened about four years ago, during the war. One day a tramp came to my office. When I looked up at him, he was standing in the door with his cap in his hands, looking as if he wanted to apologize for being on earth.

I was about to offer him a quarter when he startled me by pulling a little brown-covered booklet out of his pocket. It was a copy of *How to Build Self-Confidence*. He said, "It must have been the hand of fate that slipped this little booklet into my pocket yesterday afternoon. I was on my way to punch a hole in Lake Michigan when someone gave me this book. I read it. It caused me to stop and think, and now I am satisfied that, if you will, you can put me back on my feet again."

I looked the tramp over again. He was about the worst-looking specimen of humanity I have ever seen. He wore a two weeks' growth of beard. His clothes were unpressed and ragged. He wore no collar. His shoes were run down at the heels. But, he had come to me for help that I could not refuse. I asked him to come in and sit down. Frankly, I had not the slightest idea that I could do anything for him, but I did not have the heart to tell him so.

I asked him to tell me his story, to tell me what brought him down to that station in life. He told me his story. Briefly, it was this: Prior to the war, he was a successful manufacturer up in the state of Michigan. The war caused his factory to fail. It wiped out his savings and his business, and the blow broke his heart. It undermined his faith in himself, so he left his wife and children and went out and became a beggar.

After I had heard this story, I thought of a plan for helping him. I said to him, "I have listened to your story with a great deal of interest, and I wish I could do something for you, but there is absolutely nothing that I can do."

I watched him for a few seconds. He turned white and looked as if he were about to faint. Then I said, "But, there is a man in this building to whom I will introduce you, and that man can put you back on your feet in less than six months if you will rely upon him." He stopped me and said, "For God's sake, lead me to him." I took him out into my laboratory and stood him in front of what looked to be a curtain over a door. I reached over and pulled the curtain aside, and he stood face to face with the person to whom I had promised to introduce him, looking himself squarely in the face, in a tall looking glass.

I pointed my finger at the glass and said, "There is the only person on earth who can help you, sir; and unless you sit down and become acquainted with the strength back of that personality, you might just as well go ahead and 'punch a hole in Lake Michigan' because you will be no good to yourself or to anyone else."

He walked over real close to the glass, rubbed his bewhiskered face, then stepped back, and tears began to trickle down his cheeks.

I led him to the elevator and sent him away, never expecting to see him again.

About four days later, I met him on the streets of Chicago. A complete transformation had taken place. He was walking at a rapid pace with his chin up in the air at a forty-five-degree angle. He was dressed from head to foot with new clothes. He looked like success, and he walked as if he felt like success. He saw me and came over and shook hands.

He said, "Mr. Hill, you have changed the whole course of my life. You have saved me from myself by introducing me to myself—to my real self—the one I did not know before—and one of these days, I am coming back to see you again. When I do, I am going to be a successful man. I am going to bring you a check. Your name will be filled in at the top, and my name will be filled in at the bottom. The amount will be left blank, for you to fill in, because you have marked the biggest turning point in my life."

He turned and disappeared in the crowded streets of Chicago. As I watched him go, I wondered if I would ever see him again. I wondered if he would really make good. I just wondered and wondered. It seemed almost like reading some tale from the Arabian Nights.

Which brings me to the end of my introductory remarks, and to an appropriate place to say that this man has come back to see me again. He made good. If I mentioned his name in these columns, you would recognize it immediately, because he has attained phenomenal success and placed himself at the head of a business that is known from coast to coast.

I am trying to get him to tell his own story in these columns, that others may profit by his example. I hope I will succeed, because there are millions of others who have lost faith in the only person on this earthly plane who can do anything for them, just as this man had done, who might find themselves through his own story.

In the meantime, following is the article which brought about this unusual transformation in a man who had fallen to the lowest depths of despondency.

This can prove to be the most valuable book you ever read. It shows you how to make application of the principles of auto-suggestion and concentration in developing the most necessary of all qualities for success, self-confidence.

There are two great objects for which all humanity seems to be striving. One is to attain happiness, and the other is to accumulate material wealth—money!

TRUE!

You will begin to see the importance of developing self-confidence when you stop to realize that neither of these two chief objects of life can be achieved without it.

Try as hard as you wish, and you cannot be happy unless you believe in yourself! Work with all the strength at your command, and you cannot accumulate more than barely enough to live on unless you believe in yourself!

The one and only person in all this world through whose efforts you can be supremely happy under all circumstances, and through whose labor you can accumulate all the material wealth that you can use legitimately, is yourself.

When you come into a full realization of this great truth, a new, vibrant feeling of inspiration will seize you, and you will become conscious of a tremendous amount of vitality and power which you did not know that you possessed before.

You will accomplish more because you will dare to undertake more! You will realize, possibly for the first time in your life, that you possess the ability to accomplish anything that you wish to accomplish! You will realize how little your success in any undertaking will depend upon others and how much it will depend upon you.

We recommend that you purchase a copy of Emerson's *Essays* and read "Self-Reliance." It will fill you with new inspirations, enthusiasm, and determination.

Then, after you have read the essay on self-reliance, read the one on compensation. In these two essays, you will find some remarkably helpful truths.

In the development of self-confidence, one of the first steps you must take is to dispel forever the feeling that you cannot accomplish anything you undertake. Fear is the chief negative that stands between you and self-confidence, but we shall show you how to scientifically eliminate fear and develop courage in its place.

Reposing in your brain is a sleeping genius which can never be aroused except through the exercise of self-confidence. When it is once aroused, you will be amazed at what you can accomplish. You will surprise all who knew you before your transformation took place. You will brush aside all obstacles and sweep on to victory, backed by an invisible force which recognizes no obstacles.

A careful analysis of the successful men of the world shows that the dominating quality which they all possessed was self-confidence.

The purpose of this chart is to show you how you may, through the principles of auto-suggestion and concentration, place any thought or desire in your conscious mind and hold it there until it becomes crystallized into reality. These principles are scientific and accurate. They have been tested thousands of times by leading scientists of the world. To prove their accuracy, you have only to try them out, as hundreds of others are doing, by memorizing the following chart:

1. I know that I have the ability to accomplish all that I undertake. I know that to succeed, I have only to establish this belief in myself and follow it with vigorous, aggressive action. I will establish it.

2. I realize that my thoughts eventually reproduce themselves in material form and substance and become real in the physical state. Therefore, I will concentrate upon the daily task of thinking of the person I intend to be and of drawing a mental picture of this person and of transforming this picture into

reality. (Here describe in detail your "chief aim" or the life-work you have selected.)

3. I am studying with the firm intention of mastering the fundamental principles through which I may attract to me the desirable things of life. Through this study, I am becoming more self-reliant and more cheerful. I am developing more sympathy for my fellow men, and I am becoming stronger, both mentally and physically. I am learning to smile the smile that plays upon the heart as well as upon the lips.

4. I am mastering and overpowering the habit of starting something that I do not finish. From this time forward, I will first plan all that I wish to do, making a clear mental picture of it, and then I will let nothing interfere with my plans until I have developed them into realities.

5. I have clearly mapped out and planned the work that I intend to follow for the ensuing five years. I have set a price upon my services for each of the five years, a price that I intend to command through strict application of the principle of efficient, satisfactory service!

6. I fully realize that genuine success will come only through strict application of the "Golden Rule" principles. I will, therefore, engage in no transaction which does not benefit alike all who participate in it. I will succeed by attracting to me the forces that I wish to use. I will induce others to serve me because of my willingness to serve them. I will gain the friendship of my fellow men because of my kindness and my willingness to be a friend. I will eliminate from my mind fear by developing in its place courage. I will eliminate skepticism by developing faith. I will eliminate hatred and cynicism by developing love for humanity.

7. I will learn to stand upon my feet and express myself in clear, concise, and simple language, and to speak with force and enthusiasm, in a matter that will carry conviction. I will cause others to become interested in me, because I will first become

interested in them. I will eliminate selfishness and develop in its place the spirit of service.

Let us particularly direct your attention to the second paragraph of this self-confidence building chart. Under this heading, you must clearly and definitely state the "chief aim," and by deliberately placing it in your conscious mind, you are making use of the principle of auto-suggestion, and by memorizing this chart and holding its contents in readiness so you may call it into the conscious mind at any minute, and by actually calling it into your consciousness many times a day, you are making use of the principle of concentration.

There is a sure way to avoid criticism—be nothing and do nothing.

Get a job as a street sweeper and kill out ambition. The remedy never fails.

Your mind may be likened to the sensitive plate of a camera. The "chief aim" held before your mind, through the foregoing chart, may be likened to the object of which you wish to make a clear, definite picture. When this picture becomes transferred permanently to the sensitive plates of your subconscious mind, you will notice that every act and every movement of your body will have a tendency toward transforming this picture into a physical reality.

Your mind first draws a picture of that which it wants, and then it proceeds to direct your bodily activity toward acquiring it.

Keep fear away from your conscious mind as you would keep poison out of your food, for it is the one barrier that will stand between you and self-confidence.

After you have committed this self-confidence building chart to memory, make a habit of repeating it aloud at least twice a day. All of your thoughts have a tendency, within themselves, to produce appropriate or corresponding activities in your body, but thoughts which are followed by affirmation through spoken words will crystallize into reality in much less time than those which are not followed by expression in words. Going still further, thoughts which are followed by both spoken and written words will crystallize into physical reality in still less time than those which are inhibited and merely held in consciousness silently. Therefore, we not only strongly recommend that you will memorize this self-confidence building chart, but we also suggest that you write it out and repeat it aloud at least twice a day for at least two weeks. By following these suggestions, you will have taken three decided steps toward realizing your goal:

First, you will have created it in thought.

Second, you will have caused this to produce bodily action tending toward its ultimate transformation into reality, through the muscular action of the vocal organs in speaking aloud.

Third, you will have caused this thought to actually begin the process of transformation into physical reality through the muscular action of your hand in writing it out on paper.

These three steps would complete your task entirely in many lines of work, for example, in architecture. The architect first thinks, paints a clear picture of his building on the sensitive plates of his mind, then transfers this picture to paper with his hand, and lo! his work is completed.

We recommend that you stand before a looking glass where you can see yourself as you repeat the words of the self-confidence building chart. Look yourself squarely in the eyes as though you were some other person, and talk with vehemence. If there is any feeling of lack of courage, shake your fist in the face of that person you see in the glass and arouse him to a feeling of reaction. Make him want to say something; make him want to do something.

Soon you will actually see the lines on your face begin to change from an expression of weakness to one of strength. You will commence to see strength and beauty in that face which you never saw before, and this wonderful transformation will be quite as noticeable to others.

You need not follow the exact wording of the self-confidence building chart, but select words which more appropriately express your desire. As a matter of fact, you may write an entirely new chart if you prefer. The wording is immaterial as long as it clearly defines the picture which you intend to transform into reality.

Look upon this chart as being a blueprint or detailed description of the person you intend to be. Record in the blueprint every emotion which you wish to feel, every act which you wish to perform, and a clear description of yourself as you wish others to see you. Remember that this chart is your working plan, and that in time—a very short time at that—you are going to resemble this plan in every detail.

Let this chart become your daily prayer, if you are religiously inclined, and repeat it as such. If you believe in prayer—as you undoubtedly do—you cannot doubt for one moment that your desires, as expressed through the chart, will be fully realized. Do you not see what a remarkable position of strength you will be placed in by repeating this chart as a prayer? Do you not see with wonderful clearness just what the added quality of faith will do toward quickly and surely transforming your affirmations into physical realities? Do you not see great possibilities of this method of using the power of the Infinite for the achievement of your desires?

It makes no difference what your religion may be; this method of self-development in no way conflicts with it. People of all religions recognize prayer as the central power around which their creeds are built. If prayer has the endorsement of all religions, it must be worthy of employment in the achievement of legitimate ends. Surely the development of self-confidence is a legitimate and worthy end.

We may not be able to explain the wonderful phenomenon of prayer, but that should not prevent us from making every possible legitimate use of it. To make use of it in the transformation of the written words of the chart into physical reality surely is a legitimate use, because the purpose of this chart is the development of man, the greatest and most wonderful handiwork of God.

⇒〔What could be more worthy purpose than that of freeing the human mind from the greatest of all curses, fear? And, what is the self-confidence building chart for except to eliminate fear and build courage in its place? 〕

By making use of this chart in the manner indicated, do you not see how one is placed in the anomalous position of being compelled to develop self-confidence or doubt the power of prayer and aspiration? Do you not see what a powerful impetus is given to your undertaking by the added quality of faith which attaches to prayer?

You need not confine your chart to the development of self-confidence exclusively. Add to it any other quality that you wish to develop, happiness for example, and it will bring you what you order. To deny this is to deny the power of prayer itself.

You are now in possession of the great pass key that will unlock the door to whatever you wish yourself to be. Call this great key whatever you wish. Consider it in the light of a purely scientific force if you choose; or, look upon it as a Divine Power, belonging to the great mass of unknown phenomena which mankind has not yet fathomed. The result in either case will be the same, success.

If prayer is good for anything at all, surely it may be used as a medium through which to develop in the human mind the greatest of all blessings, happiness. You will never enjoy greater happiness than that which you will experience through the development of self-confidence. Through this method of self-confidence building, your Creator stands sponsor for your success. Do you not see what a tremendous advantage you are giving yourself through this procedure? Do you not see how impossible it will be for you to fail? Do you not see how prayer itself becomes your chief ally?

Faith is the foundation upon which civilization rests. Nothing seems impossible when built upon faith as the cornerstone to your self-confidence building. Make use of it, and your building cannot fall. You will overcome all obstacles, and tear down all resistance in accomplishing your purposes, through this simple plan. Let no prejudices stand in the way of your using this plan. To doubt that it will bring you that which you desire is the equivalent of doubting prayer.

The great curse of the ages is fear or lack of self-confidence. With this evil removed, you will see yourself being rapidly transformed into a person of strength and initiative. You will see yourself breaking out of the ranks of that great mass which we call followers, and moving up into the front row of that select few which we call leaders. Leadership only comes through supreme belief in self, and you know how to develop that belief.

Remember this as my parting shot at you—that you can be anything that you deeply and emotionally desire to be. Find out what you desire most, and you have then and there laid the foundation for acquiring it. Strong, deeply seated desire is the beginning of all human achievement—it is the seed, the germ from which all man's accomplishments spring.

Emotionalize or vitalize your whole being with any well-fixed, definite desire, and immediately your personality becomes a magnet that will attract to you the object of that desire.

To doubt is to remain in ignorance.

Environment and Habit

*T*his lesson brings us to the next general principle of psychology, which we will state as follows.

Environment: The human mind has a decided tendency to absorb the environment with which we are surrounded, and to cause bodily activity which harmonizes with and is appropriate to that environment. The mind feeds on and grows to resemble the sense impressions which it absorbs from the environment in which we live. The mind resembles a chameleon in that it changes its color to correspond to its environment. None but the strongest minds will resist the tendency to absorb the surrounding environment.

Habit: Habit grows out of environment—out of doing the same thing in the same way repeatedly—out of thinking the same thoughts over and over—and when once formed, it resembles cement which has set in the molds and is hard to break.

The force of education is so great that we may mold the minds and manners of the young into what shape we please and give the impressions of such habits as shall ever afterward remain.

—BISHOP FRANCIS ATTERBURY, 1663–1732

The human mind draws the material out of which thought and action are built from the surrounding environment, and habit crystallizes these into permanent fixtures of our personality and stores them away in our subconscious minds.

Habit may be likened to the grooves on a phonograph record, while the human mind may be likened to the needle point that fits into that groove. When any habit has been well formed (by repetition of thought or action), the mind has a tendency to attach itself to and follow that habit as closely as the phonograph needle follows the groove in the wax record.

We begin to see, therefore, the importance of selecting our environment with the greatest possible care, because it is the mental feeding grounds out of which the stuff that goes into our minds is to be extracted.

Environment supplies the food and the materials out of which we create thought, and habit crystallizes these materials into permanency!

For this very reason, under our present system of handling criminals, we make more of them than we cure! When the subjects of environment and habit are better understood, our entire penal system will receive a well-deserved overhauling and transformation. We will stop penning men together, like so many cattle, all branded with the stripe of disgrace that ever reminds them that they are "criminals"! We will place offenders in a clean atmosphere where every part of the environment will suggest to them that they are being transformed into useful human beings instead of placing them where they are constantly reminded that they are offenders of society. In this age of advancement and human intelligence, the prison ought to be considered a hospital in which perverted and deranged mentalities are nursed back to normal. The old idea of punishment for crime ought to be replaced by the new and more advanced idea of cure for crime. The law of retaliation, suggestion, auto-suggestion, and the other principles covered by this course will each play its part in doing away with punishment and adopting cure as a means of transforming criminals back to normal.

The honor system, as adopted in a limited way in many of our penal institutions, is a step in the right direction. The parole system is another step forward. The time is rapidly approaching when every offender of the laws of society will be sent, not to dark, repellant, dirty, and filthy prison cells, but directly to the laboratory of the mental hospital where the mind as well as the body of the unfortunate one will receive attention and proper treatment.

This reform in prison methods is going to be one of the great reforms of the present age! And, psychology is going to be the medium through which this reform will operate. In fact, after psychology becomes one of the regularly taught subjects in our public schools, the criminal tendencies which the growing child absorbs from its environment will be effectively counterbalanced, through the principles of psychology.

But we must not digress too far from the subjects of our lesson, habit and environment. Let us learn more about the characteristics of habit from the following words of Edward E. Beals, one of the world's leading psychologists.

Habit

"Habit is a force which is generally recognized by the average thinking person, but which is commonly viewed in its adverse aspect to the exclusion of its favorable phase. It has been well said that all men are 'the creatures of habit,' and that 'habit is a cable; we weave a thread of it each day, and it becomes so strong that we cannot break it.' But the above quotations only serve to emphasize that side of the question in which men are shown as the slaves of habit, suffering from its confining bonds. There is another side to the question, and that side shall be considered in this chapter.

"If it be true that habit becomes a cruel tyrant, ruling and compelling men against their will, desire, and inclination—and this is true in many cases—the question naturally arises in the thinking mind whether this mighty force cannot be harnessed and controlled in the service of man, just as have other forces of nature. If this result can be accomplished, then man may master habit and set it to work, instead of being a slave to it and serving it faithfully, though complaining. And the modern psychologists tell us in no uncertain tones that habit may certainly be thus mastered, harnessed, and set to work, instead of being allowed to dominate one's actions and character. And thousands of people have applied this new knowledge and have turned the force of habit into new channels, and have compelled it to work their machinery of action, instead of being allowed to run to waste, or else permitted to sweep away the structures that men have erected with care and expense, or to destroy fertile mental fields.

"A habit is a 'mental patch' over which our actions have traveled for some time, each passing making the path a little deeper and a little wider. If you have to work over a field or through a forest, you know how natural it is for you to choose the clearest path in preference to the less worn ones, and greatly in preference to stepping out across the field or through the woods and making a new path. And the line of mental action is precisely the same. It is movement along the lines of the least resistance—passage over the well-worn path.

"Habits are created by repetition and are formed in accordance to a natural law, observable in all animate things, and some would say in inanimate things as well. As an instance of the latter, it is pointed out that a piece of paper, once folded in a certain manner, will fold along the same lines the next time. And all users of sewing machines, or other delicate pieces of mechanism, know that as a machine or instrument is once 'broken in,' so will it tend to run thereafter. The same law is also observable in the case of musical instruments. Clothing or gloves form into creases according to the person using them, and these creases, once formed, will always be in effect, notwithstanding repeated pressings. Rivers and streams of water cut their courses through the land and, thereafter, flow along the habit-course. The law is in operation everywhere.

"The above illustrations will help you to form the idea of the nature of habit and will aid you in forming new mental paths—new mental creases. And remember this always—the best (and one might say the only) way in which old habits may be removed is to form new habits to counteract and replace the undesirable ones. Form new mental paths over which to travel, and the old ones will soon become less distinct and, in time, will practically fill up from disuse. Every time you travel over the path of the desirable mental habit, you make the path deeper and wider, and make it so much easier to travel it thereafter. This mental path-making is a very important thing, and I cannot urge upon you too strongly the injunction to start to work making the desirable mental paths over which you wish to travel. Practice, practice, practice—be a good path-maker.

"The following rules will help you in your work in forming new habits:

1. At the beginning of the formation of a new habit, put force into your expression of the action, thought, or characteristic. Remember that you are taking the first steps toward making the new mental path, and it is much harder at the first than it will be afterwards. Make the path as clear and deep as you can at the start, so that you can see it readily the next time you wish to travel it.

2. Keep your attention firmly concentrated on the new path building, and keep your eyes and thoughts away from the old paths, lest you incline toward them. Forget all about the old paths, and concern yourself only with the new one that you are building.

3. Travel over your newly made path as often as possible. Make opportunities for doing so, without waiting for them to arise. The oftener you go over the new path, the sooner will it become an old, well-worn, easily traveled one. Think out plans for passing over it and using it at the start.

4. Resist the temptation to travel over the older, easier paths that you have been using in the past. Every time you resist a temptation, the stronger do you become, and the easier will it be for you to do so the next time. But cvcry time you yield to the temptation, the easier does it become to yield again, and the more difficult does it become to resist the next time. You will have a fight on at the start, and this is the critical time. Prove your determination, persistency, and willpower now, right here at the start.

5. **Be sure that you have mapped out the proper path—plan it out well, and see where it will lead you to—then go ahead without fear and without allowing yourself to doubt. 'Place your hand upon the plow, and look not backward.' Select your goal—then make a good, deep, wide mental path leading straight to it."**

repose!!

There is a close resemblance between habit and auto-suggestion. Through habit, an act repeatedly performed in the same manner has a tendency to become permanent, and eventually we perform the act automatically and without much thought or concentration. In playing a piano, for example, the player can play a familiar piece while his or her conscious mind is on some other subject.

Through auto-suggestion, as we have already learned from previous lessons, a thought, idea, ambition, or desire held constantly in the mind eventually claims the greater portion of the conscious mind and, accordingly, causes appropriate muscular action of the body to the end that the idea so held may be transformed into physical reality.

Auto-suggestion, therefore, is the first principle we use in forming habits. We form habits through the principle of auto-suggestion, and we can destroy habits through the same principle.

THIS

All that you need to do in forming or eliminating any habit is to make use of the principle of auto-suggestion with persistence. A mere fleeting wish is not auto-suggestion at all. An idea or desire, to be transformed into reality, must be held in the conscious mind faithfully and persistently until it begins to take permanent form.

What is needed is a steady, determined, persistent application to the one object upon which you have set your mind. Having found the object of your desire and knowing how to concentrate upon it, you should then learn how to be persistent in your concentration, aim, and purpose.

There is nothing like sticking to a thing. Many men are brilliant, resourceful, and industrious, but they fail to reach the goal by reason of their lack of "stick-to-it-iveness." One should acquire the tenacity of the bull dog, and refuse to be shaken off a thing once he has fixed his attention and desire upon it. You remember the old Western hunter who, when once he had gazed upon an animal and said, "You're my meat," would never leave the trail or pursuit of that animal if he had to track it for weeks, losing his meat in the meantime. Such a man would, in time, acquire such a faculty of persistence that the animals feel like Davy Crockett's coon who cried out, "Don't shoot, mister, I'll come down without it."

You know the dogged persistence inherent in some men that strikes us as an irresistible force when we meet them and come into conflict with their persistent determination. We are apt to call this the "will," but it is our old friend persistence—that faculty of holding the will firmly up against objects, just as the workman holds the chisel against the object on the wheel, never taking off the pressure of the tool until the desired result is obtained.

No matter how strong a will a man may have, if he has not learned the art of persistent application of it, he fails to obtain the best results. One must learn to acquire that constant, unvarying, unrelenting application to the object of his desire that will enable him to hold his will firmly against the object until it is shaped according to his wishes. Not only today and tomorrow, but every day until the end.

Sir Thomas Fowell Buxton has said, "The longer I live, the more certain I am that the great difference between men, between the feeble and the powerful, the great and the insignificant, is energy— invincible determination—a purpose once fixed, and then death or victory. That quality will do anything that can be done in this world— and no talents, no circumstances, no opportunities, will make a two-legged creature a man without it."

Donald G. Mitchell said, "Resolve is what makes a man manifest, not puny resolve, not crude determinations, not errant purposes—but that strong and indefatigable will which treads down difficulties and danger, as a boy treads down the heaving frost-lands of winter, which kindles his eye and brain with proud pulse-beat toward the unattainable. Will makes men giants."

Disraeli said, "I have brought myself, by long meditation, to the conviction that a human being with a settled purpose must accomplish it, and that nothing can resist a will which will stake even existence upon its fulfillment."

Sir John Simpson said, "A passionate desire and an unwearied will can perform impossibilities, or what may seem to be such to the cold and feeble."

And John Foster adds his testimony when he says, "It is wonderful how even the casualties of life seem to bow to a spirit that will not bow to them, and yield to observe a design which they may, in their first apparent tendency, threaten to frustrate, when a firm, decisive spirit is recognized; it is curious to see how the space clears around a man and leaves him room and freedom."

Abraham Lincoln said of General Grant, "The great thing about him is cool persistency of purpose. He is not easily excited, and he has got the grip of a bull dog. When he once gets his teeth in, nothing can shake him off."

Now, you may object that the above quotations relate to the will, rather than to persistence. But if you stop to consider a moment, you will see that they relate to the persistent will, and that the will without persistence could accomplish none of these things claimed for it. The will is the hard chisel, but persistence is the mechanism that holds the chisel in its place, firmly pressing it up against the object to be shaped, and keeping it from slipping or relaxing its pressure. You cannot closely read the above quotations from these great authorities without feeling a tightness of your lips and setting of your jaw, the outward marks of the persistent, dogged will.

If you lack persistence, you should begin to train yourself in the direction of acquiring the habit of sticking to things. This practice will establish a new habit of the mind, and will also tend to cause the appropriate brain cells to develop and, thus, give to you as a permanent characteristic the desired quality that you are seeking to develop. Fix your mind upon your daily tasks, studies, occupation, or hobbies, and hold your attention firmly upon them by concentration, until you find yourself getting into the habit of resisting "sidetracking" or distracting influences. It is all a matter of practice and habit. Carry in your mind the idea of the chisel held firmly against the object it is shaping, as given in this lesson—it will help you so much. And read this over and over again, every day or so, until your mind will take up the idea and make it its own. By so doing, you will tend to arouse the desire for persistence, and the rest will follow naturally, as the fruit follows the budding and flowering of the tree.

Persistence may be compared to the "drop of water which finally wears away the hardest stone." When the final chapter of your lifework is written, you will find that your persistence, or lack of it, has played a mighty part for your success or failure.

In hundreds of thousands of cases, the talents of men could be matched, one against the other, with the result that there would be no noticeable difference in their ability to accomplish a desired end. One has as much education as the other. One has as much latent ability as the other. They go forth into the world with equal chances of winning the goal for which they aim, but one succeeds and the other fails! Accurate analysis will show that the one succeeded because of persistence, while the other failed because he lacked persistence!

Persistence, auto-suggestion, and habit are a trio of words, the meaning of which no one can afford to overlook. Persistence is the strong cord which binds auto-suggestion and habit together until they merge into one and become a permanent reality.

The chief strategic value of the German propaganda lies in the fact that it breaks down the spirit of those against whom it is directed. In other words, it breaks down the persistence! The Prussian who was sent to destroy the author of these lessons and render his educational work unimportant made extensive use of this principle of destroying his persistence by breaking his spirit. Silently and subtly, this trained agent of the Kaiser set about turning the author's friends and business associates against him. Well did he know the necessity of destroying the power of persistence! To crush the spirit and break down the persistence of those who stand in his way is a strong factor in the German propagandist's work. To destroy the "morale"—in other words, the persistence—of an army is of strategic importance of great value.

Destroy the morale of an army, and you have defeated that army! The same rule applies to a smaller group of individuals, or to one person.

We can only develop persistence through absolute self-confidence! This is why we have laid so much stress upon the value of the lesson on self-confidence, and why we have commended that lesson to you as being the most important lesson of applied psychology. There is a central idea around which that lesson is built, which shows you exactly how to use whatever latent ability you have, and how to supplement this with whatever faith you have in the infinite.

Go back to that lesson and ponder over it!

Behind those simple lines, you will find the secret of achievement, the key to the mysteries of an indomitable will power! Stripped and shorn of all technicalities, you will find in that lesson "that subtle something" which will vitalize your brain and send that radiant glow through your whole body that will cause you to want to grab your hat, go out, and do something!

The greatest service that any teacher can perform for you is to cause you to arouse that sleeping genius inside of your brain and inspire it with the ambition to accomplish some worthy undertaking! It is not that which education or schooling puts in your head that will benefit you, but that which is aroused in you and put to work!

Persistence on your part will eventually arouse that indescribable something, whatever it is, and when it is once aroused, you will sweep all obstacles before you and swiftly ride on to the achievement of your desired goal, on the wings of this newly found power which you had within you all the time, but didn't know it!

And when you once discover this irresistible power which sleeps in your brain this very minute, no one on earth can again dominate you or use you as a piece of putty. You will then have discovered your tremendous mental power, just as a horse discovers his superior physical power when he once runs away, and ever afterward, you will refuse to be haltered and ridden by any human being on earth!

If you follow the plan laid down in the theme around which this magazine is built, you are sure to find this great power. You will have then come to yourself. You will have discovered the true principle through which the human race has gradually, throughout ages, risen above the animals of the lower stages of evolution.

And here seems to be an appropriate point at which to recommend another book for you to add to your library—a book which will go far toward enlightening you on the subject of the evolution of the human race. The title of the book is *The Ascent of Man* by Henry Drummond, published by James J. Pott & Co., 114 Fifth Avenue, New York.

Get this book at your local library, or better still, buy a copy from your local book store. To read and assimilate this book is to acquire a liberal education on the subject of psychology. The chapter on "The Dawn of Mind" alone is worth many times the cost of the book. We recommend this and other books which we will mention later on because they have a close relationship to the subject of environment, which we now come back to.

Environment

As we have already said, we absorb sense impressions from our surrounding environment. Environment, in the sense that we here use it, covers a very broad field. It embraces the books we read, the people with whom we associate, the community in which we live, the nature of the work in which we are engaged, the country in which we reside, the clothes we wear, the songs we sing, and the thoughts we think!

The purpose of our discussion of the subject of environment is to show its direct relationship to the personality we are developing in ourselves, and the importance of creating an environment out of which we can develop the "chief aim" on which we have set our hearts!

The mind feeds upon that which we supply it through our environment; therefore, let us select our environment with the direct object of supplying the mind with suitable material out of which to carry on its work of realizing our "chief aim."

If your environment is not to your liking, change it! The first step to be taken is to create in your own mind an exact picture of the environment in which you believe you could do your best work, and from which you would probably draw those emotional feelings and qualities that would tend to urge you on toward your desired goal.

The first step you must take in every accomplishment is the creation, in the mind, of an exact outline or picture of that which you intend to build in reality. This is something you cannot afford to forget! This great truth applies to the building of a desirable environment just the same as it does to everything else that you desire to create.

THIS!!!

Your daily associates constitute the most important and influential part of your environment for either your progress or your retrogression. It will be of much benefit to you to select, as your associates, people who are in sympathy with your aims and ideals, and whose mental attitude inspires you with enthusiasm, determination, and ambition. If, perchance, you have on your list of associates a person who never sees anything except the negative side of life—a person who is always complaining and whining—a person who talks about failure and the shortcomings of humanity—erase such a person from your list, as soon as you possibly can.

Every word uttered within your hearing, every sight that reaches your eyes, and every sense impression that you receive in any other manner influences your thought as surely as the sun rises in the east and sets in the west! This being true, can you not see how important it is to control, as far as possible, the sense impressions which reach your mind? Can you not see the importance also of controlling, as far as possible, the environment in which you live? Can you not see the importance of reading books that deal with subjects which have a direct bearing on your "chief aim"? Can you not see the importance of talking with people who are in sympathy with you and your aims—people who will encourage you and urge you on to greater effort?

Through the principle of suggestion, every word uttered within your hearing and every sight within the gaze of your eyes is influencing your action. You are either consciously or unconsciously absorbing, assimilating, and making a part of yourself the ideas, thoughts, and acts of those with whom you associate. Constant association with evil minds will, in time, mold your own mind in conformity with that of the evil one. This is the chief reason why we should avoid "bad" company. The fact that association with disreputable people will bring you into disrepute in the minds of others is, within itself, sufficient reason for your avoiding such associates, but the more important reason why you should do this is the fact that you are constantly absorbing the ideas of your associates and making them a part of your own!

We are living in what we call the environment of a twentieth-century civilization. The leading scientists of the world are agreed that nature has been millions of years creating, through the process of evolution, our present civilized environment as it is represented by the present state of intellectual and physical development of man.

We have only to stop and consider what environment will do, in less than a score of years, that which it took nature, in her process of evolution, thousands of years to accomplish, to see the powerful influence of environment. A savage baby, reared by its savage parents, remains a savage; but that same baby, if reared by a refined, civilized family, throws off its savage tendencies, and all but a few of its savage instincts, absorbing its civilized environment in one generation.

On the other hand, the race descends as rapidly as it ascends, through the influence of environment. In war, for example, refined men, who, under ordinary circumstances, would shudder at the thought of killing a human being, become enthusiastic slayers, actually taking delight in the act. It requires but a few months of preparation in a "war environment" to take a man backward in evolution to where we found the Indians when we took control of North America, as far as his willingness to kill is concerned.

The clothes you wear influence you; thereby, they form a part of your environment. Soiled or shabby clothes depress you and lower your self-confidence, while clean, modest, and refined clothes give you a sort of inner feeling of courage that causes you to quicken your step as you walk. We need not tell you what a difference there is in the way you feel in your work clothes and your Sunday clothes, for you have noticed this difference many a time. In the one, you want to shrink away from people who are better dressed than you, and in the other, you meet people on an equal basis, with courage and self-confidence. Therefore, not only do others judge us by our clothes at first meeting, but we judge ourselves to a large extent by our clothes. As evidence of this, witness the feeling of discomfort and depression that we experience if our under-clothing is soiled, even though our other garments are in perfect trim and of the latest design, and our under-clothes cannot be seen.

Women spend relatively more for under-clothing than they do for outer garments, and even though the under-clothing cannot be seen by anyone except themselves, they will spend days and even weeks of laborious toil on fancy stitching and laces for the under-clothes. This seems to have considerable bearing on our subject when we stop to consider that women have far more pride, if not in fact more mental courage, than men possess. The extra frills and the additional touch of art which women add to their clothes plays its part—and a mighty strong part at that—in accounting for the superior briskness of a woman's step, her superior agility, and her traditional grace of movement.

While we are on the subject of clothes, I want to relate an experience I once had which brought home to me very forcefully the tremendous part which clothes play in one's mental courage or lack of it. I was once invited into the laboratory of a well-known teacher of physical culture. While I was there, he persuaded me to take off my clothes and accept, gratis, a simple treatment. After the treatment was over, I was ushered into his presence by an attendant, in a well-appointed office, wearing nothing except the pair of trunks in which I had taken my treatment. On the opposite side of a large mahogany desk sat my friend, the teacher of physical culture, attired in a neat formal business suit. The contrast between him and me was so great and so unavoidably noticeable that it embarrassed me. I felt a great deal like I imagine the near-sighted man felt who once made the mistake of stepping out of his dressing room into a crowded ballroom, thinking that he was going into a closet where his clothes were.

It was no mere accident that I was ushered into the presence of this teacher in scanty attire! He was a practical psychologist, and he well knew the effect it would have on a prospective purchaser of his course in physical culture to be placed at such a disadvantage. The reception had been "staged," in other words, and the chief actor who was very efficiently directing the play was the man on the other side of the desk who had on proper clothes.

With this setting, this teacher canvassed me to purchase his course, which I did. After I got back into my regular clothes and into my usual environment and analyzed the visit, I could plainly see that the sale was an easy matter under the setting which this man had very ingeniously prepared.

Good clothes affect us in two ways. First, they give us greater courage and more self-confidence, which alone would justify us in providing ourselves with proper clothes, even to the exclusion of some other necessity of less value. Second, they impress others in our favor. The first sensory impression which reaches the mind of those whom we meet reaches them through the sense of sight as they quickly look us over and take mental inventory of our wearing apparel. In this way, a person often forms an opinion of us, good, bad, or indifferent, before we utter a word, based entirely upon the impression which our clothes and the manner in which we wear them make upon his mind.

Money invested in good clothes is not a luxury but a sound business investment that will pay the best of dividends. We simply cannot afford to neglect our personal appearance, both for the effect it will have on us and for the effect it will have upon those with whom we come in contact socially, commercially, or professionally, according to our calling. Good clothes are not an extravagance—they are a necessity! These statements are based upon scientifically sound principles. The most important part of our physical environment is that which we create by the clothes we wear, because this particular part of our environment affects both ourselves and all with whom we come in contact.

Next to our clothes, an important factor in the surroundings which constitute our environment is the office or shop in which we work. Experiments have proved conclusively that a workman is influenced very decidedly by the harmony, or lack of it, which surrounds him during his working hours. A disorganized, chaotic, dirty shop or office tends to depress a workman and lower his enthusiasm and his interest in his work, whereas a well-organized, clean, and systematic work place has just the opposite effect.

Employers who, in recent years, have come to understand how to employ the principles of psychology to increase the efficiency of their employees have learned the advantage, in dollars and cents, of providing clean, comfortable, harmonious shops and offices.

Among the devices installed by the more progressive employers, as a means of increasing the enthusiasm and efficiency of their employees, are playgrounds, tennis courts, well-appointed restrooms, libraries and reading rooms equipped with pictures and statuary which tend to produce a condition of serenity in the employees' minds.

One unusually progressive laundryman of Chicago has plainly outdone his competitors, particularly in times when help is hard to get, by installing in his workroom an electric player piano and a neatly dressed young woman who keeps it going during the working hours.

ning room is located on the street floor, and the neat
nce of his women workers, dressed in white uniforms—
caps and aprons—together with their bright, cheerful faces, is one of
his best advertisements, to say nothing of the increased work which
each woman performs under these harmonious surroundings.

Contrast this scene with the appearance of the average laundry,
where the women are uncouth in appearance and the workroom
disorganized and presenting an appearance of a rag picker's shop, and
you will readily see the advantage of the more progressive system, an
advantage that takes into consideration both increased profits to the
employer and greater comfort of the employee.

The time is not far ahead when some sort of music will be
considered a necessity in every shop where men and women are
working with their hands. Music produces harmony and enthusiasm,
both of which are essential if the maximum efficiency is obtained by
the workman. A man cannot be highly efficient unless he loves his
work and his environment—his working surroundings. With the
right selection of music, a workman's production could be increased
from ten to fifty percent, without fatiguing him in the least.

During war times, when most of the workers of America are
engaged in the manufacture of war materials of one sort and another,
think of the inspiration, the increased strokes a man could strike, the
greater number of steps he could make if he were keeping time with
"Over There" or with some other soul-stirring music, such as
"Dixie" or "Yankee Doodle"! Under such conditions, a man could
easily double his production in many lines of work and still feel less
fatigued at night!

If you doubt that music makes one oblivious to time and effort,
just study people who are dancing or roller-skating to a tune of good
music. A person will dance or skate until twelve o'clock at night, after
having performed a hard day's work at the shop or office, and still feel
perfectly fresh for the next day's work, if supplied with good music.

We stop to wonder sometimes why it is that more employers do
not learn a lesson from the dancer or the skater and make use of the

same psychology, to stimulate the workers' efforts in shop or office, that carries the dancers and skaters through hours of the hardest sort of physical labor without any way of fatiguing them!

The more competent of the "efficiency engineers" have not been slow to grasp the importance of making use of this psychology in laying out plans for working conditions in shops and offices. Whenever increased human efficiency takes place at all, it begins in the human mind! Men produce greater results because they want to do so! Now, the problem is to find ways and means, devices and equipment, environment and surroundings, atmosphere and working conditions with which to make men and women want to do more work and better work!

Environment is the first thing the really efficient "efficiency counselor" takes cognizance of. A man cannot be a competent efficiency counselor without being also a psychologist.

I am thoroughly convinced, after taking a retrospective view of my experience as a boy on a farm, that if I were engaged in the business of farming and had to depend upon boys to help me do the work, I would provide a baseball ground nearby and such other games as boys like to engage in, and every so often, we would finish a given task or a pre-arranged piece of work, and then sally forth to the ball ground for a little turn at the "enthusiasm builder"!

With this incentive with which to look forward, a boy (and most of us are only boys grown tall) would produce more work and experience less fatigue than he would without it. That old axiom, "all work and no play makes Jack a dull boy" is more than an axiom—it is a scientific truth with teeth in it!

Somewhere, sometime, some foreman, superintendent, or manager of men, or perhaps some individual workman, will read this lesson and see the practical value of entertaining men while they work and of providing them with a pleasing, harmonious environment. Not only will he see the practical value of the idea, but better still, he will put it into use and make it carry him into prominent leadership!

Perhaps you are that man or woman!

If you have faithfully put into practice the suggestions laid down in the lesson on self-confidence building, you are undoubtedly headed in the direction of leadership. What you now need is some big idea with which to complete the journey. It may be that on these pages you will find that idea!

One big idea is all that any person really needs or can make use of in this life. Too many of us go through life with plenty of little ideas clinging to us, but with no really big idea! When you find your big idea, more likely than not, you will find it in some sort of service that will be of constructive help to your fellowmen! It may be the idea of lowering the cost to the consumer of some necessity of life; or, it may be the idea of helping men and women to discover the wonderful power of the human mind and how to make use of it; or, it may be the idea of helping men and women to be more cheerful and happy in their work by creating some plan for improving their working environment. If it doesn't promise some of these results, you may be reasonably sure that it is not a big idea.

Throughout the industrial and commercial world, there is a prevailing spirit of unrest among the workmen. Probably the greatest worldwide problem now confronting the human race is this question of unrest among the workers. Both the leaders of labor and the leaders of finance are cognizant of the widespread and growing dissatisfaction among workmen, and both are equally aware that the problem must have immediate and wise counsel.

What an opportunity this situation offers for someone to create his big idea! Fame and fortune await the man who solves any part of the great problem which the spirit of unrest among workmen presents to the world. When that problem is solved, either in whole or in part, the question of providing a congenial environment in which workmen may labor will surely play an important part.

It may be that in this subject of unrest among workmen, you will find your big idea. What more worthy cause could you devote your life to than that of helping to improve the environment of those who earn their living with their hands? What wonderful satisfaction comes to those whose big idea is found in that great field of endeavor wherein we strive to make others happy as they tarry by the wayside of life!

It may be that this field of effort does not always yield as great a return in dollars and cents, but certain it is that its workers enjoy that serene, harmonious mental environment which is always experienced by those who give their lives for the uplift and the enlightenment of humanity. Incidentally, this brings us to a suitable point at which to discuss the last phase of environment, which is mental environment.

Up to this point, we have been discussing the purely physical side of environment, such as the clothes we wear, the equipment with which we work, the room in which we work, the people with whom we associate, and the like. As between the mental and the physical sides of environment, the mental side is of greater importance. Our mental environment is represented by the condition of our minds. In the last analysis, the physical environment is merely the material out of which we create our mental environment. The exact state of mind existing at any given time is the result of sense impressions which have reached the mind from the physical environment, at one time or another, and constitutes our mental environment.

We can rise above and beyond a negative physical environment by creating in our imagination a positive one, or by shutting out all thought of it altogether, but a negative mental environment cannot be dodged—it must be rebuilt. Out of our mental environment, we create every impulse to bodily action; therefore, if our muscular, bodily activities are wisely directed, they must emanate from a sound mental environment. Hence, we claim that as between the mental and physical environments, the former is of greater importance.

❧

Summary

We have learned from this lesson the part which environment and habit play in one's success or failure. We have learned that there are two phases of environment, one mental and the other physical, and that the mental side is created out of the physical. We have learned, therefore, the importance of controlling, as far as possible, the physical environment, because it is the raw material out of which we build the mental environment.

We have learned how to make and to unmake habit, through persistence and auto-suggestion. We have learned that both auto-suggestion and concentration play an important part in the creation of any habit.

We have learned that the tendency of the human mind is to absorb its surrounding environment and to pattern after it its impulses to muscular, bodily action. We have learned, therefore, that environment is the raw material out of which we are shaping our ideas and our characters. We have learned that so forceful is the environment in which we live that a sound mind may absorb criminal tendencies by improper association with criminal minds, through inadequate penal institutions, etc.

We have learned that the clothes we wear constitute an important part of our physical environment, and that they influence us as well as those with whom we come in contact, either negatively or positively, according to their appropriateness.

We have learned the importance of providing workmen with a pleasing, harmonious physical environment and of the increased efficiency that may be produced by so doing.

The Easy Road
G.S.W.

How many seek the gladness,
   That love and friendship lend,
Forgetting to be friendly,
   While asking for a friend.
How many seek position
   And highest tasks to do,
And strive to rule the many
   While faithless to the few.

How many fix their vision
   On mountains lost in light,
Yet scorn the weary climbing
   That leads them to the height.
And choosing false conditions,
   How many then complain,
Because life's laws are changeless
   And truth and justice reign.
Because, as to Mohammed,
   Life teaches to each one
That all may seek the mountain,
   That mountain comes to none.

To every sincere, inquiring mind, Nature declares, "Tell me what you want. I can get it for you." But the majority do not know what they want; nor do they want the same thing twice in succession. That is why more dreams do not come true. Adopt a "chief aim" in life.

How to Remember

The principles through which accurate, organized memory may be cultivated compose one of the chief major subjects of psychology.

What a wonderful "gift" is that of a perfect memory—the ability to recall both names and faces of people whom we have met, and of sense impressions which have reached our subconscious minds through what we call "experience."

We need not try to convince you that a reliable memory is an asset, because you already know this. Let us hasten, then, to a discussion of the three chief principles of memory, which are briefly defined as follows:

1. *Retention*—The receiving of the sense impression through one or more of the five senses and the recording of this impression in the subconscious mind. This process may be likened to the recording of a picture on the sensitized plate of a camera.

2. *Recall*—The reviving again of those sense impressions which have been recorded in the subconscious mind, and bringing them into the conscious mind. This process may be compared to the act of going through a card index and pulling out a card on which data had been previously recorded.

3. *Recognition*—The ability to recognize a sense impression when it is called into the conscious mind, and to identify it as being a duplicate of the original. This enables us to distinguish between "memory" and "imagination."

How to Make Effective Use of These Three Principles

First: Make the first impression vivid by concentrating your attention upon it to the finest detail. Just as the photographer takes care to give an "exposure" proper time to record on the sensitized plate of the camera, so must we give the subconscious mind time to properly record any sense impression which we wish to be able to recall with readiness.

Second: Associate that which you wish to remember with some object, name, or place with which you are quite familiar and which you can recall at any time without effort as, for example, your home town, your mother, your close friend, etc.

Third: Repeat that which you wish to remember a number of times, at the same time concentrating your mind upon it. The great failing of not being able to remember names, which most of us have, is due entirely to the fact that we do not properly record the name in the first place. When you are introduced to a person whose name you wish to be able to recall instantly, stop and repeat his or her name two or three times, first making sure that you understood the name correctly.

An accurate memory is something which you can acquire in exactly the same manner that the photographer acquires accuracy in his art, namely, by properly exposing the negative so that all of the features, outlines, lights, and shades of the object photographed are recorded on the sensitized plates of your subconscious mind!

There are many exclusive courses on the subject of memory training, some of which have been padded out in considerable length. All you need, however, is to grasp the fundamental principles through which the memory functions, and soon you can develop an accurate memory. To do this, you need not follow any formula too closely, but rather invent your own method. Some remarkably accurate memories have been developed through the use of the principle of concentration alone.

Rules and formulas are confusing. The best method to follow is to get a clear understanding of the fundamental principles through which memory can be developed, and then apply these principles in your own way. The following will illustrate the comparative simplicity with which one man developed an accurate memory.

How I Brought Back a Wandering Mind

"I am fifty years old. For a decade, I have been a department manager in a large factory. At first, my duties were easy; then the firm had a rapid expansion of business which gave me added responsibilities. Several of the young men in my department developed unusual energy and ability—at least one of them had his eye on my job.

"I had reached the age in life when a man likes to be comfortable, and having been with the company a long time, I felt that I could safely settle back into an easy berth. The effect of this mental attitude was well-nigh disastrous to my position.

"About two years ago, I noticed that my power of concentration was weakening, and my duties were becoming irksome. I neglected my correspondence until I looked with dread upon the formidable pile of letters; reports accumulated, and subordinates were inconvenienced by the delay. I sat at the desk with my mind wandering elsewhere.

"Other circumstances showed plainly that my mind was not on my work; I forgot to attend an important meeting of the officers of the company. One of the clerks under me caught a bad mistake made in an estimate on a carload of goods and, of course, saw to it that the manager learned of the incident.

"I was thoroughly alarmed at the situation and asked for a week's vacation to think things over. I was determined to resign, or find the trouble and remedy it. A few days of earnest introspection at an out-of-the-way mountain resort convinced me that I was suffering from a plain case of wandering mind. I was lacking in concentration; my physical and mental activities at the desk had become desultory. I was careless and shiftless and neglectful—all because my mind was not alertly on the job. When I had diagnosed my case with satisfaction to myself, I next sought the remedy. Evidently, I needed a complete new set of working habits, and I made a resolve to acquire them.

"With paper and pencil, I outlined a schedule to cover the working day: first, the morning mail, then the orders to be filled, dictation, conference with subordinates, and miscellaneous duties, ending with a clean desk before I left.

"'How is a habit formed?' I asked myself mentally. 'By repetition,' came back the answer. 'But I have been doing these things over and over thousands of times,' the other fellow in me protested. 'True, but not in orderly, concentrated fashion,' replied the echo.

"I returned to the office with mind in leash, but restless, and placed my new working schedule into force at once. I performed the same duties with the same zest and, as nearly as possible, at the same time every day. When my mind started to slip away, I quickly brought it back.

"From a mental stimulus, created by will power, I progressed in habit building. Day after day, I practiced concentration of thought. When I found repetition becoming comfortable, then I knew that I had won."

Please keep constantly in mind the fact that this is a course in "applied" psychology, and that its chief purpose is to give you a good grasp of those qualities through which you may attain success in all of your undertakings.

We shall make no attempt in this course to adhere to the old methods of pedagogy. You have started out to acquire information concerning the human mind and to ascertain the relationship between the mind and your business of succeeding in your life work. You want practical, applied psychology instead of theoretical psychology! You want to understand the relationship between the principles of psychology and the business of earning a living and of being happy while you are doing it!

We feel it our duty to you, therefore, to go outside of our psychological laboratory for data with which to illustrate the principles of psychology. We feel it our duty to you to show you just how the principles covered by this course have actually worked out, in a practical business world. In doing this, we feel at liberty to draw upon the experiences of men who have used these principles, and to pass on to you the results. In quoting the following story, we are passing on to you a remarkable example of the advantage of an accurate memory as well as some very simple methods through which to cultivate such a memory.

A Great Businessman with a Wonderful Memory

"America has a man with a wonderful memory, developed by close observation, lively imagination, and indomitable industry and perseverance.

"The geography of every country is lined in his mind as cleanly as the streets of his native town in Connecticut. He carries in his mind a moving picture of the whole earth. The cartoonist could fittingly portray him by substituting the globe for his head.

"He is neither a ship owner nor a captain, yet he has a practical knowledge of a shipping business comparable with that of any living ship owner or skipper.

"He is neither a customs official nor a professional tariff expert, yet he carries in his head information in great detail on national and international tariffs and customs duties.

"In the great organization of which he is president, there are two hundred and seventy thousand employees—yes, two hundred and seventy thousand, or more than the population of St. Paul or Louisville or Denver or Atlanta.

"He sits at his desk in New York and talks with the operating and commercial officials identified with this vast industry, one-third across the continent, making suggestions and recommendations having to do with the multitudinous details of the largest industrial organization in the world.

"His list of engagements to see people at times averages from forty to fifty every day, or between twelve hundred and fifteen hundred every month, aside from which he contrives to carry on an extensive correspondence.

"He is familiar with every minute phase of his concern's manufacturing and selling business, a business that is running at a rate of three million dollars a day, or not very far from a billion dollars a year.

James A. Farrell's Wonderful Memory

"Questioned once on the witness stand as to what ingredients enter into wine products, he replied, 'Between two and three hundred. Shall I name them?' Again asked, 'How many competitors has the American Bridge Company, one of your subsidiaries?' he replied, 'Three hundred and sixty-eight,' and occupied one morning giving their locations, capacities, and character of work produced by them.

"Asked, among thousands of other questions, whether the shipping facilities to certain parts of South America were good or bad, he immediately replied, 'One hundred and fifty-eight vessels left here for the River Plate last year, sufficient for the volume of tonnage offered.'

"This living gazetteer of the world, this walking atlas, this international encyclopedia, this commercial wizard, this industrial phenomenon, is James A. Farrell, ex-laborer, now president of the United States Steel Corporation.

"For ten days, Mr. Farrell sat in the witness chair during the government's suit against the steel corporation and, without consulting books, papers, or data of any kind, answered every question fired at him. Not once did he have to reply, 'I don't know.' He appeared to know everything, and to remember everything. Here, for example, is his reply—made wholly without any notes or memoranda—to the question, 'Can you remember what percentage of the business of each of the subsidiaries of the steel corporation was foreign in 1910 and in 1912?'

"'Yes, the Carnegie Steel Company, 21 percent in 1910, 24 percent in 1912; the National Tube Company, 10 percent in 1910, 12 percent in 1912; the American Sheet and Tin Plate Company, 11 percent in 1910, 20 percent in 1912; the American Steel & Wire Company, 17 percent in 1910, 20

percent in 1912; the Lorain Steel Company, 30
percent in both periods; the American Bridge
Company, 6 percent in 1910, 8.5 percent in 1912;
the Illinois Steel Company, 1.2 percent in 1910, 2.4
percent in 1912.'

"The judge and everybody gasped.

" 'That man's mind is a self-working cash register
and adding machine combined,' remarked one of
the attorneys.

"Mr. Farrell's uncanny knowledge of steel making
and steel selling—he worked years in the mills in
many departments of the industry and years on the
road as salesman; his unparalleled knowledge of
shipping and of overseas countries—he first went
voyaging with his father, who was captain of a
Maine-built ship, when twelve, and has since
traveled in many lands; his familiarity with foreign
tariffs and trade conditions all over the world—all
this he has turned into profitable account for
himself and still more for his country by increasing
his company's export sales of iron and steel
products from less than $3,000,000 a dozen years
ago to over $100,000,000 during the last year, an
achievement in international trade not matched by
any other American of the past or the present.

The Steel President Talks about
Acquiring a Good Memory

" 'To cultivate a good memory,' according to Mr.
Farrell, 'at first requires effort—great effort. In time,
it becomes easy and natural to remember things. To
retain things in your mind becomes a habit.

" 'Sir Arthur Conan Doyle, in his writing, propounded the right idea. You must concentrate. You must not carry any useless mental baggage. You must concentrate on the things in which you are interested and expunge from your memory everything you are not interested in. There must be not only a spring cleaning, but a daily cleaning of your memory, so to speak, in order to make room for fresh stores of helpful information.

" 'James J. Hill, who had perhaps one of the most remarkable memories of any man in the country, used to say that it is easy to remember things in which one is interested. Anyone wishing to acquire comprehensive knowledge of his business, or of any specific subject, must not try to store his mind with endless details about other things. For example, I have tried to learn all I could about the steel business in its mining, manufacturing, selling, and transportation branches, but to enable me to carry business information in my head, I have not attempted to retain in my mind minute detailed data about politics or baseball.

" 'Absorb what to you is essential—that is, everything pertaining to your field of endeavor. Abolish from your mind nonessential, extraneous subjects. No human brain has cells enough to store up all the facts about all subjects under the sun. Don't clog your brain cells with impedimenta. Feed them only with vital material, with things that will enhance your usefulness in your sphere of activity by increasing and improving your stock of needful information.'

" 'How can a young man start in to improve his memory?' I asked.

A Tip to Young Businessmen

" 'The best foundation on which to build a strong memory is to cultivate a capacity for work. Good habits also contribute to a good memory; careless habits tend to distract and spoil the memory. A clear head is necessary to a keen memory.

" 'It is essentially true of the mind that it grows on what it feeds. Youth is the time when the mind and memory are most sensitive, most retentive, and most plastic. It is especially important, therefore, to begin the proper training of the mind at an early age. It is as difficult to dislodge cumbersome, useless things from the mind as it is to acquire new and better supplies of knowledge. What was done badly has to be undone—often at considerable cost. As with most worthwhile things in this world, a good memory calls for the paying of a price. Any youth or man who desires to train his memory must be prepared to pay the cost. He must be prepared to forgo an endless round of even harmless pleasures. He must not hope to shine continually and conspicuously in social or society circles during his formative years. He must study while others play. His reading must be limited very largely to books and magazines and papers which will help him to acquire facts and a better understanding of whatever business or subjects he is determined to master. He must utilize most of his spare time and not idle it away.

" 'Although I worked twelve hours a day when I started as a laborer in a wire mill when I was only fifteen years old, I studied very hard after finishing the whole round of the clock daily in the mill. I tried to learn all I could about the making of wire, and I managed to qualify as a mechanic in a little over a year. I interested myself not only in the making of wire and in the general manufacturing of iron and steel, but I had a fondness for selling things, and I did my best to learn all about the duties of a salesman. When I did become a salesman, I found my experience in the mill and my knowledge of the manufacturing end of the business a most valuable asset when I went to call on buyers.

" 'At school, I found it easy to learn geography. My father and grandfather were both seafaring men, and maybe this helped to turn my attention to other parts of the world and to broaden my vision. It was natural that I should consider the possibilities of foreign outlets for steel products, so that before I became a foreign sales manager, I had studied the subject very earnestly. Being interested, I could remember what I read and learned. Today, I suppose I do know a fair amount about foreign markets for steel and transportation facilities— how to reach these markets.

" 'The opening up of foreign markets for American products has entailed, of course, a great deal of detail work. But having accustomed my memory to retaining details, the work has appealed to me and has not been so very difficult to handle.'

"It is recognized throughout the steel industry that 'Jim' Farrell has no peer as a master of detail. His oral replies to the government's lawyers made their heads swim. They could not stump him, try as they might. John D. Rockefeller used to impress upon his aides that, next to knowing one's own business, the most important thing to know was what the other fellow was doing. Mr. Farrell abundantly demonstrated that he not only knew what his own corporation and every other company in the United States was doing, but he was as familiar with iron and steel activities in other countries as with the process of manufacturing wire.

The Importance of Knowing All about Your Job

"Some executives declare, airily, that they never bother about details, that they do not know anything about them and leave their handling entirely to subordinates. I was anxious to get from Mr. Farrell his view of the importance of a knowledge of details and having them properly attended to. My question struck a responsive chord.

" 'I could conceive no more humiliating experience,' he replied, 'than to be asked some question concerning our operations and to be obliged to send for a subordinate to answer it. I would not consider myself fit for the job unless I knew the ins and outs of the business and how each detail of it is conducted.

" 'Suppose a manager of one of our properties were to be confronted suddenly with some problem, and were to call me up direct from the mills or mines for advice; wouldn't I feel extremely foolish if I couldn't grasp what he was talking about, and realize exactly the conditions facing him there?

" 'This corporation has many officers in the producing and selling departments. Not only do I

meet and talk with many of them periodically in my office here, or during my frequent visits to our different properties, but I take pains to give their communications proper attention.

" 'If you were manager of an important enterprise and wrote a letter to the owner about something of importance, you would not like to receive a perfunctory reply from John Smith, one of his secretaries. In the same way, if the president or other officer of a subsidiary refers anything to me for my particular consideration, I would reduce the value and dampen the enthusiasm of that man were I to turn the matter over to John Smith.' "

We have reprinted this whole story because it is full of inspiration that will be of help to you. It is the equivalent of a good course in memory training, but it is more—much more than this—it is an ambition builder that will be sure to cause you to want to accomplish something that is worthwhile!

One of the chief objects of this course is to arouse in you that "vital spark" which we refer to by various names, such as determination, ambition, etc., and cause it to develop into a flame of enthusiasm that will carry you on to a greater achievement of some sort!

You are sure to find, somewhere in this magazine, the loose ends of the threads of life which lead to your desired goal! You are sure to get hold of at least one big idea that you can nourish and develop into a finished product that will bring you success and happiness. Just which one of these chapters you will find this idea in, or whether you will find it in more than one, we cannot say. You may find this idea in a single word or a single sentence. We wish that we might point out to you the exact chapter, the paragraph, and the sentence in which this idea is to be found, but this is impossible, because some will find it in one place, while others will find it somewhere else.

You will have to find it for yourself, and when you do, you will readily recognize it. We know that it is here, because this magazine covers all of the principles through which the human mind works, and the human mind is first cause for all that any person ever accomplished or ever will accomplish.

Through this course in applied psychology, you have gone back to the first cause of all the power that man has or can use in any sort of achievement. You are at the fountainhead from which all human achievements are drawn! It makes no difference what life work you have selected, or what work you intend to follow; you will have to make use of the principles which are covered by this course; therefore, in the study of the course, you are preparing yourself for success in whatever field of endeavor the future may find you engaged in.

We want you to get this viewpoint, because it will help you to search diligently and with intense interest for the "end of the thread" which, when unwound, will lead you to your desired station in life.

As a befitting close for this chapter on memory, we quote the following from the work on applied psychology by Dr. Warren Hilton, author of *Applied Psychology* (12-volume set) and founder of the Society of Applied Psychology.

A Scientific Memory System
for Business Success

"We recall things by their associates. When you set your mind to remember any particular fact, your conscious effort should be not vaguely to will that it should be impressed and retained, but analytically and deliberately to connect it with one or more other facts already in your mind.

"The student who 'crams' for an examination makes no permanent addition to his knowledge. There can be no recall without association, and 'cramming' allows no time to form associations.

"If you find it difficult to remember a fact or a name, do not waste your energies in 'willing' it to return. Try to recall some other fact or name associated with the first in time or place or otherwise, and lo! when you least expect it, it will pop into your thoughts.

"If your memory is good in most respects, but poor in a particular line, it is because you do not interest yourself in that line and, therefore, have no material for association. Blind Tom's memory was a blank on most subjects, but he was a walking encyclopedia on music.

"To improve your memory, you must increase the number and variety of your mental associations.

"Many ingenious methods, scientifically correct, have been devised to aid in the remembering of particular facts. These methods are based wholly on the principle that that is most easily recalled which is associated in our mind with the most complex and elaborate groupings of related ideas.

"The same principle is at the basis of all efficient pedagogy. The competent teacher endeavors by some association of ideas to link every new fact with those facts which the pupil already has acquired.

"In the pursuit of this method, the teacher will compare all that is far off and foreign to something that is near home, making the unknown plain by the sample of the known, and connecting all the instruction with the personal experience of the pupil—if the teacher is to explain the distance of the sun from the earth, let him ask, 'If anyone here in the sun fired off a cannon straight at you, what should you do?' 'Get out of the way,' would be the answer. 'No need of that,' the teacher might reply; 'you may quietly go to sleep in your room and get up again, you may wait till your confirmation day, you may learn a trade, and grow as old as I am—then only will the cannonball be getting near; then you may jump to one side! See, so great as that is the sun's distance!'

"We shall now show you how to apply this principle in improving your memory and in making a more complete use of your really vast store of knowledge.

"Rule I: MAKE SYSTEMATIC USE OF YOUR SENSE ORGANS.

"Do you find it difficult to remember names? It is because you do not link them in your mind with enough associations. Every time a man is introduced to you, look about you. Who is present? Take note of as many and as great a variety of surrounding facts and circumstances as possible. Think of the man's name, and take another look at his face, his dress, his physique. Think of his name, and mark the place where you are now for the first time meeting him. Think of his name in conjunction with the name and personality of the friend who presented him.

"Memory is not a distant faculty of mind in the sense that one man is generously endowed in that respect while another is deficient. Memory, as meaning the power of voluntary recall, is wholly a question of trained habits of mental operation.

"Your memory is just as good as mine or any other man's. It is your indifference to what you call 'irrelevant facts' that is at fault. Therefore, cultivate habits of observation. Fortify the observed facts you wish to recall with a multitude of outside associations. Never rest with a mere halfway knowledge of things.

"To assist you in training yourself in those habits of observation that make a good memory of outside facts, we append the following exercises:

"(a) Walk slowly through a room with which you are not familiar. Then make a list of all the contents of the room you can recall. Do this every day for a week, using a different room each time. Do it not half-heartedly, but as if your life depended on your ability to remember. At the end of the week, you will be surprised at the improvement you have made.

"(b) As you walk along the street, observe all that occurs in a space of one block, things heard as well as things seen. Two hours later, make a list of all you can recall. Do this twice a day for ten days. Then compare results.

"(c) Make a practice of recounting each night the incidents of the day. The prospect of having this to do will cause you unconsciously to observe more attentively.

"This is the method by which Thurlow Weed acquired his phenomenal memory. As a young man with political ambitions, he had been much troubled by his inability to recall names and faces. So he began the practice each night of telling his wife the most minute details that had occurred during the day. He kept this up for fifty years, and it so trained his powers for observation that he became as well known for his unfailing memory as for his political adroitness.

"(d) Glance once at an outline map of some state. Put it out of sight and draw one as nearly like it as you can. Then compare it with the original. Do this frequently.

"(e) Have someone read you a sentence out of a magazine, and you then repeat it. Do this daily, gradually increasing the length of the quotation from short sentences to whole paragraphs. Try to find out what is the extreme limit of your ability in this respect compared with that of other members of your family.

"Rule II: FIX IDEAS BY THEIR ASSOCIATES.

"There are other things to be remembered besides facts of outside observation. You are not one whose life is passed entirely in a physical world. You live also within. Your mind is unceasingly at work with the materials of the past, painting the pictures of the future. You are called upon to scheme, to devise, to invent, to compose, and to foresee.

"If all this mental work is not wasted energy, you must be able to recall its conclusions when occasion requires. A happy thought comes to you— will you remember it tomorrow when the hour of action arrives? There is but one way to be sure, and that is by making a study of the whole associative mental process.

"Review the train of ideas by which you reached your conclusion. Carry the thought on in mind to its legitimate conclusion. See yourself acting upon it. Mark its relations to other persons.

"Note all the details of the mental picture. In other words, to remember thoughts, cultivate sense-observation to remember outside matters.

"To train yourself in thought-memory, use the following exercises:

"(a) Every morning at eight o'clock sharp on the minute, fix upon a certain idea and determine to recall it at a certain hour during the day. Put your whole will into this resolution. Try to imagine what activities you will be engaged in at the appointed hour, and think of the chosen idea as identified with those activities. Associate it in your mind with some object that will be at hand when the set time comes. Having thus fixed the idea in your mind, forget it. Do not refer to it in your thoughts. With practice, you will find yourself automatically carrying out your own orders. Persist in this exercise for at least three months.

"(b) Every night when you retire, fix upon the hour at which you wish to get up in the morning. In connection with your waking at that hour, think of all the sounds that will be apt to be occurring at that particular time. Bar every other thought from your consciousness and fall asleep with the intense determination to arise at the time set. By all means, get up instantly when you awaken. Keep up this exercise, and you will soon be able to awaken at any hour you may wish.

"(c) Every morning, outline the general plan of your activities for the day. Select only the important things. Do not bother with the details. Determine upon the logical order for your day's work. Think not so much of how you are to do things as of the things you are to do. Keep your mind on results. And having made your plan, stick to it. Be your own boss. Let nothing tempt you from your set purpose. Make this daily planning a habit and hold to it through life. It will give you a great lift toward whatever prize you seek.

"Rule III: SEARCH SYSTEMATICALLY AND PERSISTENTLY.

"When once you have started upon an effort at recollection, persevere. The date or face or event that you wish to recall is bound up with the multitude of other facts of observation and of your mind life of the past. Success in recalling it depends simply upon your ability to hit upon some idea so indissolubly associated with the object of search that the recall of one automatically recalls the others. Consequently, the thing to do is to hold your attention to one definite line of thought until you have exhausted its possibilities. You must pass in review all the associated matters and suppress or ignore them until the right one comes to mind. This may be a short-cut process or a round-about process, but it will bring results nine times out of ten and, if habitually persisted in, will greatly improve your power of voluntary recall.

"Rule IV: THE INSTANT YOU RECOLLECT A THING TO BE DONE, DO IT.

"Every idea that memory thrusts into your consciousness carries with it the impulse to act upon it. If you fail to do so, the matter may not occur to you, or when it does, it may be too late.

"Your mental mechanism will serve you faithfully only as long as you act upon its suggestions.

"This is as true of bodily habits as of business affairs. The time to act upon an important matter that just now comes to mind is not 'tomorrow' or 'a little later,' but now.

"What you do from moment to moment tells the story of your career. Ideas that come to you should be compared as to their relative importance. But do this honestly. Do not be swayed by distracting impulses that inadvertently slip in. And having gauged their importance, give free rein at once to the impulse to do everything that should not make way for something more important.

"If, for any reason, action must be deferred, fix the matter in your mind to be called up at the proper time. Drive all other thoughts from your consciousness. Give your whole attention to one matter. Determine the exact moment at which you wish it to be recalled. Then put your whole self into the determination to remember it at precisely the right moment. And, finally, and perhaps most important of all—

"Rule V: HAVE SOME SIGN OR TOKEN.

"This memory signal may be anything you choose, but it must, somehow, be directly connected with the hour at which the main event is to be recalled.

"Make a business of observing the memory signs or tokens you have been habitually using. Practice tagging those matters you wish to recall with the labels that form a part of your mental machinery.

"Make it a habit to do things when they ought to be done and in the order in which you ought to do them. Habits like this are 'paths' along which the mind 'moves,' paths of least resistance to those qualities of promptness, energy, persistence, accuracy, self-control, and so on, that increase success.

"Success in business, success in life, can come only through the formation of right habits. A right habit can be deliberately acquired only by doing a thing consciously until it comes to be done unconsciously and automatically.

"Every man, consciously or unconsciously, forms his own memory habits, good or bad. Form your memory habits consciously according to the laws of the mind, and in good time, they will act unconsciously and with masterful precision.

" 'Amid the shadows of the pyramids,' Bonaparte said to his soldiers, 'twenty centuries look down upon you,' and animated them to action and victory. 'But all the centuries,' says W. H. Grove, 'and the eternities, and God, and the universe, look down upon us—and demand the highest culture of body, mind, and spirit.'

"A good memory is yours for the making. But you must make it. We can point the way. You must act.

"The laws of association and recall are the combination that will unlock the treasure-vaults of memory. Apply these laws, and the riches of experience will be available to you in every need."

⌒

Summary

In this lesson, you have learned that concentration on the subject to be remembered is one of the chief factors in accurate memory.

You have learned that by associating that which you wish to remember with something with which you are familiar and which you can easily recall, your ability to remember is greatly increased. You have learned that the subconscious mind classifies the sense impressions reaching your mind and files those which are similar or which bear a close association together, so that when the thing with which a sense impression is associated is called into the conscious mind, it brings with it that sense impression.

You have learned that repetition enables your subconscious mind to get a clear picture of the sense impression that you wish recorded in your memory, and that by repeating over and over the name of that which you wish to remember, you will have no trouble recalling it when wanted.

ASSOCIATION—CONCENTRATION—REPETITION are the three chief allies of memory!

You have learned that indifference at the time a sense impression is made is the chief reason for a poor memory. Next to this in the list of the three chief enemies of memory are divided attention at the time of the sense impression and lack of concentration.

You have also learned, through the story of Mr. Farrell, the relationship between an accurate memory and success in your life work.

If the subject of memory had to be defined in one short sentence, we would word that sentence as follows:

"Concentrate your full attention on that which you wish to remember, picture it in your mind, repeat it aloud, then associate it with some person or place which you can readily recall at any time."

9

How Mark Antony Used Suggestion in Winning the Roman Mob

A few years ago, I received a telephone call from the Secretary of the Press Club. He said, "This is Mr. Blank, Secretary of the Press Club. I called up to congratulate you on your being elected to membership in this club. You were voted upon and elected last night, and I will send a man out from the office this afternoon to get your signature to the application for membership."

I thanked him and, with my mouth still wide open, hung up the receiver. In an hour or so, a young man walked into my office, walked right up to my desk boldly, and laid a simple-looking little application on my desk.

He said, "The Secretary of the Press Club sent this out for your signature," and stood with his hat in his hand, waiting for me to sign. I picked up the paper, looked it over hurriedly, and started to sign, when it occurred to me that I would like to know, more out of curiosity than anything else, who had submitted my name for membership in the Press Club. I asked the young man if he knew who submitted my name, and he said that he didn't, that possibly it was some friend who already belonged to the Club. Then he hurried to explain that it was quite an honor to be elected to membership in the Club. I picked up my pen again and started to write my name on the dotted line. The application was printed on cheap paper, and the pen "stuck" in the paper, causing me to hesitate for a moment and start to write in a new place. The hesitation gave me time to think some more about who submitted my name for membership, so I stopped, laid down the pen, and asked the young man to telephone the Secretary and find out who it was. He did so, but got word back that the Secretary didn't know who submitted my name.

Here suspicion entered for the first time, so I told the young man that I believed I would not sign just then. At the same time, I read the application over again. It called for a membership fee of $150. Those figures looked ten times as big as they had looked a minute or so before that telephone conversation. I was beginning to get "cold feet." I was beginning to feel that I was about to be "sold" something. Up to this point, I had felt that I was getting into a very select Club, through the thoughtfulness of some good friend. Frankly, my vanity had overcome my better business judgment. But now I was beginning to wake up and "smell a mouse." Then the young man spoke up and said, "Why, you probably fail to appreciate how hard it is to get into the Press Club. No one can get in until he has been elected by vote. You have been paid an honor that you cannot afford to reject."

Those words sank deep. For the moment, they seemed to allay suspicion and make me feel that probably I had been rather hasty in laying down the fountain pen, so I reached for it again, but before I lifted it from the desk, I caught sight of those figures again, $150. They looked still bigger, so I pushed the application back to the young man and said, "No, I must think this over for a few days," and I ushered him to the door.

The next day, I was telling one of my friends that I had been elected to membership in the Press Club. I showed plainly by the expression on my face that I felt rather proud of the honor. Then he laughed! I had never heard him laugh so loudly in my life. He said, "Look here, if you really want to join the Press Club, I can get you a membership for $50. Frankly, I don't believe you want to belong to it, but if you do, I can save you $100." Then he continued—"It may also interest you to know that the Club is making a drive for membership just now; therefore, you needn't feel so 'chesty' about having been elected to membership!"

I began to grow small! I remember the feeling distinctly. I will never forget it. Down, down, down I went in the scale of intelligence, until I can remember how I had to look straight up to see my friend, even though I was as tall as he.

Then I saw the joke. I took my friend to the cigar counter and bought him a box of the best Havanas I could purchase. "What are these for?" he asked, in surprise. And I replied, "In payment for the best lesson in salesmanship that I ever had or ever will have."

You now have the story, which I have told to every member of our class in Advertising and Salesmanship. It hurts my pride to tell this story, but it is so valuable to a student of applied psychology that I simply could not pass by the opportunity to tell it.

My vanity had almost cost me $150. The only thing that saved me was the poor grade of paper on which the Press Club application was printed. If the pen hadn't "stuck," I would have been! That was a real case of "letting me buy" instead of "selling me." I was doing all the buying. No one asked me to join the Club. I was virtually ready, not only to join and part with $150 in cash, but to thank someone for "giving me the opportunity." Here was the weak part of their sales plan—they lost my confidence when they failed to tell me who submitted my name for membership. The man who planned that sales plan was "almost" a master salesman. He fell down in just that one slight detail. It would have been all right had they said to me that the Club had been watching my business progress and had decided that I would be a good man for membership, but when they refused to assure me on this point, I lost confidence and they lost the signature on the little dotted line.

I need not analyze this story for you. The psychology back of it is so plain that a schoolboy can understand it. Use this psychology yourself. As to just how you may do this will depend upon the problem in hand. It will depend upon the buyer and the commodity which you have to sell.

This same principle of psychology was used by Mark Antony in his wonderful oration, which you will read presently. In this oration, you will see how adroitly he appealed to the vanity of the Roman mob. Did he start out by trying to "sell" them on his viewpoint? No, not he! He was too clever a salesman for that. Study his oration carefully. Get the big thought back of it. See how Mark Antony, figuratively speaking, floated with the stream and not against it, until he came to a point of vantage where he could turn its course in the direction that he wanted it to go.

It is necessary to handle a thousand tons of clay and dross in order to obtain a milligram of radium! The process of separation is a long, tedious, and expensive one, but that is the only way to secure radium. That is one reason why radium is so expensive.

To get at a seemingly simple truth, we must sometimes go through masses of evidence, sorting out the usable from the unusable, but it must be done if we want the "radium." There is a simple truth in connection with applied psychology which is the very warp and woof of all successful salesmanship; therefore, when you get through reading this lecture, if you feel that I have taken you through the radium refining process to get at this great truth, I know you will also be fair enough to admit that the time spent in the search has been well worthwhile.

I will not tell you what this great truth is, now. I want you to have the benefit of finding it yourself. In bringing out this great principle, I am going to make use of Shakespeare's remarkable oration which he put into the mouth of Mark Antony, in his reply to Brutus, over the dead body of Caesar. Nothing which I have ever read portrays one of the underlying principles of applied psychology as well as this oration.

The same psychological laws and principles used by Antony in his oration over the body of Caesar will bring as great a measure of success, and as effectually win the day now as it did before the fall of Brutus.

As I proceed with the text of the oration, I shall inject between the lines certain comments for the purpose of bringing out more clearly the comparison I wish to make.

❧

Argument of the Scene

Caesar has been killed, and Brutus has just finished his address to the populace, setting forth his reasons for Caesar's removal. These reasons have been accepted, and the mob believed in him. Brutus was probably the most admired and most beloved man in all Rome at that time. Hence, his simple statement was accepted with equally simple faith.

Here, Shakespeare introduces both sides of the question, first through Brutus, and then through Antony.

Brutus, having presented his side, and satisfied that he has won the day, closes his speech and rests his case. But he had not fully convinced his audience. The Roman mob was not well sold. Over-confident, he yielded the platform to Antony too soon. Nevertheless, the mob was with him and against anyone who had aught to say derogatory to him.

Antony appears upon the scene, with the mob at least partly antagonistic to him and suspicious, lest he be against Brutus. His first step is to pacify them and get their minds in a receptive condition (to neutralize their minds) for, without this, he cannot make any headway. He must also avoid all appearance of "knocking" the other side. These are essentials in convincing an audience or an individual; your audience must be presumed to be open to conviction, and you should not "knock."

ANTONY: "For Brutus' sake, I am beholding to you." (Goes into pulpit.)

FOURTH CITIZEN: "What does he say of Brutus?"

THIRD CITIZEN: "He says, for Brutus' sake, he finds himself beholding to us all."

FOURTH CITIZEN: "'Twere best he speak no harm of Brutus here."

FIRST CITIZEN: "This Caesar was a tyrant."

THIRD CITIZEN: "Nay, that's certain; we are blest that Rome is rid of him."

SECOND CITIZEN: "Peace! Let us hear what Antony can say."

ANTONY: "You gentle Romans,—"

ALL: "Peace, ho! Let us hear him."

At this point, the average amateur usually tears this oration to tatters by strutting to the front of the stage, throwing out his chest, and in a tone twice too large for his body, shouting, "Friends, Romans, countrymen!"

Had Antony addressed the mob in this wise, the history of Rome would not be what it is today. For the purpose of pacifying their inflamed minds, he begins:

ANTONY: "Friends, Romans, countrymen, lend me your ears; I come to bury Caesar, not to praise him." (Conciliation.) "The evil that men do lives after them; the good is oft interred with their bones; so let it be with Caesar. The noble Brutus hath told you Caesar was ambitious; if it were so, it was a grievous fault, and grievously hath Caesar answer'd it. Here, under leave of Brutus and the rest,—For Brutus is an honorable man; so are they all honorable men,—come I to speak in Caesar's funeral. He was my friend, faithful and just to me." (Whatever he may have been to you, he was just to me; therefore, I admired him.)—

"But Brutus says he was ambitious; and Brutus is an honorable man. He hath brought many captives home to Rome, whose ransoms did the general coffers fill. Did this in Caesar seem ambitious? When the poor have cried, Caesar hath wept; ambition should be made of sterner stuff. Yet Brutus says he was ambitious; and Brutus is an honorable man. You all did see that on the Lupercal I thrice presented him a kingly crown, which he did thrice refuse; was this ambition? Yet Brutus says he was ambitious; and, sure, he is an honorable man. I speak not to disprove what Brutus spoke, but here I am to speak what I do know. You all did love him once, not without cause; what cause withholds you then to mourn for him? O judgment! thou are fled to brutish beasts, and men have lost their reason. Bear with me; my heart is in the coffin there with Caesar, and I must pause till it come back to me." (Working upon their emotions.)

He has now reached the first step in the mental law of salesman-ship. He has gained the attention of the mob. He knows that they cannot be kept entirely quiet, and so he gives them an opportunity to talk, or think, aloud. Likewise, a salesman should give his prospect an opportunity to talk early in the interview so that he, the salesman, may learn the other's weak points.

FIRST CITIZEN: "Me thinks there is much reason in his sayings."

SECOND CITIZEN: "If thou consider rightly of the matter, Caesar has had great wrong."

THIRD CITIZEN: "Has he, masters? I fear there will be worse come in his place."

FOURTH CITIZEN: "Mark'd ye his words? He would not take the crown? Therefore, 'tis certain he was not ambitious."

SECOND CITIZEN: "Poor soul! His eyes are red as fire with weeping." (Pity.)

THIRD CITIZEN: "There's not a nobler man in Rome than Antony."

FOURTH CITIZEN: "Now mark him, he begins again to speak."

ANTONY: "But yesterday, the word of Caesar might have stood against the world; now lies he there, and none so poor to do him reverence. O masters," (flattery), "if I were disposed to stir your hearts and minds to mutiny and rage, I should do Brutus wrong and Cassius wrong, who, you all know, are honorable men." (Catch the suggestion in the words *mutiny* and *rage*, the emphasis of repetition.)

From this point forward, he says three times that these are honorable men. Note the change in inflection, and the effect of each change. The first time, he makes a plain statement of fact; the second time, there is a faint suggestion of doubt as to their honesty, and the third time, with consummate skill, he plays upon the word *honorable* with such fine sarcasm and irony, as to convey to the mob the thought and idea that these men are anything but honorable.

ANTONY: "I will not do them wrong; I rather choose to wrong the dead, to wrong myself and you, than I will wrong such honorable men."

When he says he would rather wrong the dead, he knows that will excite their pity—when he prefers to wrong himself, he arouses their admiration, and when he tells them he chooses to wrong them, he stirs up their antagonism and resentment against the murder of Caesar. (He now arouses their curiosity.)

ANTONY: "But here's a parchment, with the seal of Caesar; I found it in his closet; 'tis his will; let but the commons hear his testament, which, pardon me, I do not mean to read.—And they would go and kiss dead Caesar's wounds and dip their napkins in his sacred blood, yea, beg a hair of him for memory, and, dying, mention it within their wills, bequeathing it as a rich legacy unto their issue."

FOURTH CITIZEN: "We'll hear the will; read it, Mark Antony." (Human nature wants that which is about to be taken away from it.)

Observe how craftily Antony has arrived at the second step in the mental law of salesmanship; how completely he has awakened their interest. This was done by exciting their curiosity. Of course, he intends to read the will, but he is going to compel them to demand it before he does so.

ALL: "The will, the will! We will hear Caesar's will."

ANTONY: "Have patience, gentle friends, I must not read it; it is not meet that you know how Caesar loved you. You are not wood, you are not stones, but men; and, being men, hearing the will of Caesar, it will inflame you, it will make you mad." (Just what he intends it to do.) "'Tis good you know not that you are his heirs, for if you should, O what would come of it!"

FOURTH CITIZEN: "Read the will; we'll hear it, Antony; you shall read us the will, Caesar's will."

ANTONY: "Will you be patient? Will you stay awhile? I fear I have o'ershot myself to tell you of it; I fear I wrong the honorable men whose daggers have stabb'd Caesar, I do fear it." (The words *daggers* and *stabb'd* suggest murder. See how quickly they catch the suggestion.)

FOURTH CITIZEN: "They were traitors, honorable men!"

ALL: "The will! The testament!"

SECOND CITIZEN: "They were villains, murderers; the will!"

ANTONY: "You will compel me then to read the will? Then make a ring about the corpse of Caesar, and let me show you him that made the will. Shall I descent? And will you give me leave?"

ALL: "Come down."

SECOND CITIZEN: "Descent."

THIRD CITIZEN: "You shall have leave."

SECOND CITIZEN: "Room for Antony, most noble Antony."

Beginning to feel his power over his audience, Antony now intends to get closer. He removes the barrier of distance between the pulpit and the floor of the Forum, that he may become more confidential. Observe the first note of authority, yet kindly spoken, as he commands them to stand back.

ANTONY: "Nay, press not so upon me, stand far off."

ALL: "Stand back. Room."

ANTONY: "If you have tears, prepare to shed them now, you all do know this mantle; I remember the first time Caesar put it on; 'twas on a summer's evening, in his tent, that day he overcome the Nervii." (Sentiment, love, and patriotism.)

From this point forward, he appeals to their emotional natures, to their pity for "pity is akin to love," and he desires to fan into a flame their slumbering love for Caesar.

ANTONY: "Look, in this place ran Cassius' dagger through; see what a rent the envious Casca made; through this the well-beloved Brutus stabb'd; and as he plucked his cursed steel away, mark how the blood of Caesar followed it, as rushing out of door, to be resolved if Brutus so unkindly knock'd, or no; for Brutus, as you know, was Caesar's angel; judge, O you gods, how dearly Caesar loved him! This was the most unkindest cut of all; for when the noble Caesar saw him stab, ingratitude, more strong than traitors' arms quite vanquish'd him; then burst his mighty heart; and, in his mantle muffling up his face, even at the base of Pompey's statue, while all the while ran blood, great Caesar fell, O, what a fall was there, my countrymen! Then I, and you, and all of us fell down while bloody treason flourish'd over us. O, how you weep, and I perceive you feel the dint of pity; these are gracious drops. Kind souls, why weep you when you but behold our Caesar's vesture wounded? Look you here, here is himself, marr'd, as you see, with traitors." (They have now accepted this word *traitor* and freely apply it to the conspirators.)

FIRST CITIZEN: "O piteous spectacle!"

SECOND CITIZEN: "O noble Caesar!"

THIRD CITIZEN: "O woeful day!"

FIRST CITIZEN: "O most bloody sight!"

SECOND CITIZEN: "We will be revenged."

ALL: "Revenge! About! Seek! Burn! Fire! Kill! Slay! Let not a traitor live!"

He has now attained the third step—desire. The mob desires to do that which he wished them to do. Right here, many a salesman loses his prospect. He mistakes desire for will, tries, too soon, to carry his point and frightens off the prospect who has not yet been led up to the fourth step and, consequently, is not ready to receive the salesman with open arms.

Antony, however, skilled salesman that he was, determined to carry his listeners with him; to close his argument up so tightly as to prevent the possibility of his audience being again influenced by the opposition, and so lost to him. He has saved his strongest argument and appeal for the last, so as to enable him to carry his audience with absolute certainty. Note his trump card well on toward the close of his oration:

ANTONY: "Stay, countrymen."

FIRST CITIZEN: "Peace there! Hear the noble Antony."

SECOND CITIZEN: "We'll hear him, we'll follow him, we'll die with him."

ANTONY: "Good friends, sweet friends, let me not stir you up to such a sudden flood of mutiny." (Strengthening their desire.) "They that have done this deed are honorable. What private griefs they have, alas, I know not, that made them do it; they are wise and honorable, and will, no doubt, with reasons answer you."

Observe how pregnant with double meaning are his inflections upon certain words, and how unerringly they convey to the mob his opinion of the character of the conspirators.

ANTONY: "I come not, friends, to steal away your hearts; I am not orator as Brutus is; but, as you know me all, a plain, blunt man, that love my friend; and that they know full well that gave we public leave to speak of him; for I have neither wit, nor words, nor worth, action, nor utterance, nor the power of speech to stir men's blood, I only speak right on; I tell you that which you yourselves do know; show you sweet Caesar's wounds, poor, poor, dumb mouths, and bid them speak for me; but were I Brutus and Brutus Antony, there an Antony would ruffle up your spirits, and put a tongue in every wound of Caesar that should move the stones of Rome to rise and mutiny."

ALL: "We'll mutiny."

FIRST CITIZEN: "We'll burn the house of Brutus."

THIRD CITIZEN: "Away, then! Come, seek the conspirators."

ANTONY: "Yet hear me, countrymen; yet hear me speak!"

ALL: "Peace, ho! Hear Antony. Most noble Antony!"

ANTONY: "Why, friends, you go to do you know not what; wherein hath Caesar thus deserved your love? Alas, you know not; I must tell you, then; you have forgot the will I told you of."

He has intended all along to read the will, but has held off until they were hungry for it, and their minds in a stage where the reading of it would be most effective in the accomplishment of his purpose. This was his trump card, and he saved it for the last.

Many a salesman, in his eagerness to present the merits of his goods, plays his trump card first, before his prospect is ready for it. If this does not sweep his prospect with him at the start, he can follow up with weaker points, and simmer down to a lost sale. He tries to reach the fourth step without thoroughly covering the first three, and he usually fails.

Antony now makes his appeal to the cupidity and avarice of his hearers—a common weakness of human nature.

ALL: "Most true, the will! Let's stay and hear the will."

ANTONY: "Here is the will, and under Caesar's seal. To every Roman citizen he gives, to every several man, seventy-five drachmas."

SECOND CITIZEN: "Most noble Caesar! We'll revenge his death."

THIRD CITIZEN: "O royal Caesar!"

ANTONY: "Hear me with patience."

ALL: "Peace, ho!"

ANTONY: "Moreover, he hath left you all his walks, his private arbors and new-planted orchards, on this side Tiber; he hath left them you, and to your heirs forever; common pleasures, to walk abroad and recreate yourselves, here was a Caesar! When comes such another?"

FIRST CITIZEN: "Never, never. Come, away, away! We'll burn his body in the holy place and, with the brands, fire the traitors' homes. Take up the body."

SECOND CITIZEN: "Go, fetch fire."

THIRD CITIZEN: "Pluck down benches."

FOURTH CITIZEN: "Pluck down forms, windows, anything." (Exit Citizens with the body.)

He has come to the fourth step. He has influenced their wills to do his bidding. He has carried the day.

If you will plan your sales argument along the lines upon which this oration was modeled, following it out to its conclusion as carefully, watching its development as alertly, massing your arguments in as logical an order of sequence, making each step stronger than its predecessor, sweeping aside all opposition and leaving it not ground upon which to gain a fresh foothold, keeping yourself well in hand throughout the campaign, your success will be assured.

10

Persuasion versus Force

$\mathcal{T}$he world war has done more than anything which has happened in the history of the world to show us the futility of force as a means of influencing the human mind. Without going into details or recounting the instances which could be cited, we all know that force was the foundation upon which German philosophy has been built during the past forty years. The doctrine that might makes right was given a worldwide trial, and it failed.

The human body can be imprisoned or controlled by physical force, but not so with the human mind. No man on earth can control the mind of a normal, healthy person if that person chooses to exercise his God-given right to control his mind. The majority of people do not exercise this right. They go through the world, thanks to our faulty educational system, without having discovered the strength which lies dormant in their own minds. Now and then, something happens, more in the nature of an accident than anything else, which awakens a person and causes him to discover where his real strength lies and how to use it in the development of industry or one of the professions. Result: a genius is born!

There is a given point at which the human mind stops rising or exploring unless something out of the daily routine happens to "push" it over this obstacle. In some minds, this point is very low, and in others, it is very high. In still others, it varies between low and high. The individual who discovers a way to artificially stimulate his mind, arouse it, and cause it to go beyond this average stopping point frequently is sure to be rewarded with fame and fortune if his efforts are of a constructive nature.

The educator who discovers a way to stimulate any mind and cause it to rise above his average stopping point, without any bad reactionary effects, will confer a blessing on the human race second to none in the history of the world. We, of course, do not have reference to physical stimulants or narcotics. These will always arouse the mind for a time, but eventually they ruin it entirely. We have reference to a purely mental stimulant, such as that which comes through intense interest, desire, enthusiasm, love, etc.

The person who makes this discovery will do much toward solving the crime problem. You can do almost anything with a person when you learn how to influence his mind. The mind may be likened to a great field. It is a very fertile field which always produces a crop after the kind of seed which is sown in it. The problem, then, is to learn how to select the right sort of seed and how to sow that seed so that it takes root and grows quickly. We are sowing seed in our minds daily, hourly, nay, every second, but we are doing it promiscuously and more or less unconsciously. We must learn to do it after a carefully prepared plan, according to a well-laid-out design! Haphazardly sown seed in the human mind brings back a haphazard crop! There is no escape from this result.

History is full of notable cases of men who have been transformed from law-abiding, peaceful, constructive citizens to roving, vicious criminals. We also have thousands of cases wherein men of the low, vicious, so-called criminal type have been transformed into constructive, law-abiding citizens. In every one of these cases, the transformation of the human being took place in the mind of the man. He created in his own mind, for one reason or another, a picture of what he desired and then proceeded to transform that picture into reality. As a matter of fact, if a picture of any environment, condition, or thing be pictured in the human mind, and if the mind be focused or concentrated on that picture long enough and persistently enough, and backed up with a strong desire for the thing pictured, it is but a short step from the picture to the realization of it in physical or mental form. This is a principle which we learned of in the lesson on auto-suggestion.

The world war brought out many startling tendencies of the human mind which corroborate the work which the psychologist has carried on in his research into the workings of the mind. The following account of a rough, uncouth, unschooled, undisciplined young mountaineer is an excellent case in point:

Fought for His Religion; Now Great War Hero

Rotarians Plan to Present Farm to Alva York, Unlettered Tennessee Squirrel Hunter

George W. Dixon

How Alva Cullom York, an unlettered Tennessee squirrel hunter, became the foremost hero of the American Expeditionary Forces in France forms a romantic chapter in the history of the world war.

York is a native of Fentress County. He was born and reared among the hardy mountaineers of the Tennessee woods. There is not even a railroad in Fentress County. During his earlier years, he was reputed to be a desperate character. He was what was known as a gun man. He was a dead shot with a revolver, and his prowess with the rifle was known far and wide among the plain people of the Tennessee hills.

One day, a religious organization pitched its tent in the community in which York and his parents lived. It was a strange sect that came to the mountains looking for converts, but the methods of the evangelist of the new cult were full of fire and emotionalism. They denounced the sinner, the vile character, and the man who took advantage of his neighbor. They pointed to the religion of the Master as an example that all should follow.

Alva Gets Religion

Alva Cullom York startled his neighbors one night by flinging himself down at the mourners' bench.

Old men stirred in their seats, and women craned their necks, as York wrestled with his sins in the shadows of the Tennessee mountains.

York became an ardent apostle of the new religion. He became an exhorter, a leader in the religious life of the community and, although his marksmanship was as deadly as ever, no one feared him who walked in the path of righteousness.

When the news of the war reached that remote section of Tennessee and the mountaineers were told that they were going to be "conscripted," York grew sullen and disagreeable. He didn't believe in killing human beings, even in war. His Bible taught him, "Thou shalt not kill." To his mind, this was literal and final. He was branded as a "conscientious objector."

The draft officers anticipated trouble. They knew that his mind was made up, and they would have to reach him in some manner other than by threats of punishment.

War in a Holy Cause

They went to York with a Bible and showed him that the war was in a holy cause—the cause of liberty and human freedom. They pointed out that men like himself were called upon by the higher powers to make the world free, to protect innocent women and children from violation, to make life worth living for the poor and oppressed, to overcome the "beast" pictured in the scriptures, and to make the world free for the development of

Christian ideals and Christian manhood and womanhood. It was a fight between the hosts of righteousness and the hordes of Satan. The devil was trying to conquer the world through his chosen agents, the Kaiser and his generals.

York's eyes blazed with a fierce light. His big hands closed like a vise. His strong jaws snapped. "The Kaiser," he hissed between his teeth, "the beast! The destroyer of women and children! I'll show him where he belongs if I ever get within gunshot of him!"

He caressed his rifle, kissed his mother goodbye, and told her he would see her again when the Kaiser had been put out of business.

He went to the training camp and drilled with scrupulous care and strict obedience to orders.

His skill at target practice attracted attention. His comrades were puzzled at his high scores. They had not reckoned that a backwoods squirrel hunter would make fine material for a sniper in the front line trenches.

York's part in the war is now history. General Pershing has designated him as the foremost individual hero of the war. He won every decoration, including the Congressional Medal, the Croix de Guerre, the Legion of Honor. He faced the Germans without fear of death. He was fighting to vindicate his religion for the sanctity of the home, the love of women and children, the preservation of the ideals of Christianity, and the liberties of the poor and oppressed. Fear was not in his code or his vocabulary. His cool daring electrified more than a million men and set the world to talking about this strange, unlettered hero from the hills of Tennessee.

His exploits have been given pages in newspapers and magazines. He captured a hundred Germans and herded them as he would a flock of sheep in his native mountains. He shot Germans as he had shot squirrels in Fentress County, and with as deadly aim.

Some weeks ago, a Nashville newspaper sent a reporter to the mountain home of York's mother to seek some tidings from the hero of two continents. The aged mother greeted the reporter kindly and replied that she had received a letter from Alva, that he was "getting along powerful well and getting mighty good pay." He was a private.

All this strange talk about Alva was foreign to her. What was the use of it all? Suppose he had killed lots of Germans and captured more. That was what he went over for. She could not see why they should make such a fuss about the thing like that.

Eyes of World on Alva York

But the eyes of the world are riveted on the plain mountain boy from Tennessee. He presents a study in those qualities that have come to the surface in great emergencies in American history, set up an independent nation on the shores of the Western world, conquered the wilderness, and set the flag of freedom in its most remote fastness.

The International Rotary Club has inaugurated a movement to buy and dedicate a farm to the use of

York during his lifetime. The editor of a Nashville newspaper, who is president of the Rotary Club of that city, has proposed that the youth from Tennessee be awarded something more substantial than medals for his heroism. The deed to the farm will be made out to President Wilson and then transferred to York, according to the plan proposed.

Fred T. Wilson of Houston, who was born in an adjoining county to Fentress, feels a personal pride in the exploits of his old neighbor. He says he expects to be in Nashville when Alva is given his homecoming reception. He predicts that the hero will be elected to political office in Tennessee if he will agree to serve.

Here we have a case of a young mountaineer who, had he been approached from just a slightly different angle, undoubtedly would have resisted conscription and, likely as not, would have become so embittered toward his country that he would have become an outlaw, looking for an opportunity to strike back at the first chance.

Those who approached him knew something of the principles through which the human mind works. They knew how to manage young York by first overcoming the resistance that he had worked up in his own mind. This is the very point at which thousands of men, through improper understanding of these principles, are arbitrarily classed as criminals and treated as dangerous, vicious people. Through suggestion, these people could have been handled as effectively as young York was handled and developed into useful, productive human beings.

In your search for ways and means of understanding and manipulating your own mind so you can persuade it to create that which you desire in life, let us remind you that, without a single exception, anything which irritates you and arouses you to anger, hatred, dislike, or cynicism is destructive and very bad for you.

You can never get the maximum, or even a fair average of constructive action out of your mind until you have learned to control it and keep it from becoming stimulated through anger or fear!

These two negatives, anger and fear, are positively destructive to your mind, and as long as you allow them to remain, you can be sure of results which are unsatisfactory and way below what you are capable of producing.

In our chapter on environment and habit, we learned that the individual mind is amenable to the suggestions of environment, and that the minds of a crowd blend with one another in conformity with the suggestion of the prevailing influence of the leader or dominating figure. Mr. J. A. Fisk gives us an interesting account of the influence of mental suggestion in the revival meeting which bears out the statement that the crowd mind blends into one, as follows.

∽

Mental Suggestion in the Revival

Modern psychology has firmly established the fact that the greater part of the phenomena of the religious "revival" is physical rather than spiritual in its nature, and abnormally physical at that. The leading authorities recognize the fact that the mental excitement attendant upon the emotional appeals of the "revivalist" must be classified with the phenomena of hypnotic suggestion rather than with that of true religious experience. And those who have made a close study of the subject believe that instead of such excitement tending to elevate the mind and exalt the spirit of the individual, it serves to weaken and degrade the mind and prostitute the spirit by dragging it in the mud of abnormal psychic frenzy and emotional excess. In fact, by some careful observers familiar with the respective phenomena, the religious "revival" meeting is classed with the public hypnotic "entertainment" as a typical example of psychic intoxication and hysterical excess.

David Starr Jorden, president of Leland Stanford University, says, "Whiskey, cocaine, and alcohol bring temporary insanity, and so does a revival of religion." Professor William James, of Harvard University, the eminent psychologist, says, "Religious revivalism is more dangerous to the life of society than drunkenness."

It should be unnecessary to state that in this article, the term *revival* is used in the narrower signification indicating the typical religious emotional excitement known by the term in question, and is not intended to apply to the older and respected religious experience designated by the same term, which was so highly revered among the Puritans, Lutherans, and others in the past. A standard reference work speaks of the general subject of the "revival" as follows.

> **"Revivals, though not called by that name, occurred at intervals from apostolic times till the Reformation, the revivalists being sometimes so unsympathetically treated that they left the church and formed sects; while in other cases, and notably in those of the founders of the monastic orders, they were retained and acted on the church as a whole. The spiritual impulse which led to the Reformation, and the antagonistic one which produced or attended the rise of the Society of Jesus, were both revivalist. It is, however, to sudden increase of spiritual activity within the Protestant churches that the term *revival* is chiefly confined. The enterprise of the Wesleys and Whitefield in this country and England from 1738 onward was thoroughly revivalist. Since then, various revivals have from time to time occurred, and nearly all denominations aim at their production. The means adopted are prayer for the Holy Spirit, meetings continued night after night, often to a late hour, stirring addresses, chiefly from revivalist laymen,**

and after-meetings to deal with those impressed. Ultimately it has been found that some of those apparently converted have been steadfast, others have fallen back, while deadness proportioned to the previous excitement temporarily prevails. Sometimes excitable persons at revival meetings utter piercing cries, or even fall prostrate. These morbid manifestations are now discouraged and have, in consequence, become more rare."

In order to understand the principle of the operation of mental suggestion in the revival meeting, we must first understand something of what is known as the psychology of the crowd. Psychologists are aware that the psychology of a crowd, considered as a whole, differs materially from that of the separate individuals composing that crowd. There is a crowd of separate individuals and a composite crowd in which the emotional natures of the units seem to blend and fuse. The change from the first-named crowd to the second arises from the influence of earnest attention or deep emotional appeals or common interest. When this change occurs, the crowd becomes a composite individual, the degree of whose intelligence and emotional control is but little above that of its weakest member. This fact, startling as it may appear to the average reader, is well known and is admitted by the leading psychologists of the day; and many important essays and magazines have been written thereupon. The predominant characteristics of this "composite-mindedness" of a crowd are the evidences of extreme suggestibility, response to appeals of emotion, vivid imagination, and action arising from imitation—all of which are mental traits universally manifested by primitive man. In short, the crowd manifests atavism, or reversion to early racial traits.

Gideon H. Diall, in his *Psychology of the Aggregate Mind of an Audience*, holds that the mind of an assemblage listening to a powerful speaker undergoes a curious process called "fusion," by which the individuals in the audience, losing their personal traits for the time being, to a greater or lesser degree, are reduced, as it were, to a single individual whose characteristics are those of an impulsive youth of twenty, imbued in general with high ideals, but lacking in reasoning power and will. Gabriel Tarde, the French psychologist, advances similar views.

Professor Joseph Jastrow, in his *Fact and Fable in Psychology*, says:

> **"In the production of this state of mind, a factor, as yet unmentioned, plays a leading role, the power of mental contagion. Error, like truth, flourishes in crowds. At the heart of sympathy, each finds a home. No form of contagion is so insidious in its outset, so difficult to check in its advance, so certain to leave germs that may at any moment reveal their pernicious power, as a mental contagion—the contagion of fear, of panic, of fanaticism, of lawlessness, of superstition, of error. In brief, we must add to the many factors which contribute to deception, the recognized lowering of critical ability, of the owner of accurate observation, indeed, of rationality, which merely being one of a crowd induces. The conjurer finds it easy to perform to a large audience, because, among other reasons, it is easier to arouse their admiration and sympathy, easier to make them forget themselves and enter into the uncritical spirit of wonderland. It would seem that in some respects, the critical tone of an assembly, like the strength of a chain, is that of its weakest member."**

Professor Gustave Le Bon, in his *The Crowd*, says:

> **"The sentiments and ideas of all the persons in the gathering take one and the same direction, and their conscious personality vanishes. A collective**

mind is formed, doubtless transitory, by presenting very clearly marked characteristics. The gathering has become what, in the absence of a better expression, I will call an organized crowd, or if the term be considered preferable, a psychological crowd. It forms a single being and is subjected to the law of the mental unity of crowds.

"The most striking peculiarity presented by a psychological crowd is the following: Whoever be the individuals that compose it, however like or unlike be their mode of life, their occupation, their character, or their intelligence, the fact that they have been transformed into a crowd puts them in possession of a sort of collective mind which makes them feel, think, and act in a manner quite different from that in which each individual of them would feel, think, and act were he in a state of isolation. There are certain ideas and feelings which do not come into being, or do not transform themselves into acts, except in the case of the individuals forming a crowd. In crowds, it is stupidity and not mother wit that is accumulated. In the collective mind, the intellectual aptitudes of the individuals, and in consequence their individuality, are weakened.

"The most careful observations seem to prove that an individual immersed for some length of time in a crowd in action soon finds himself in a special state which most resembles the state of fascination in which the hypnotized individual finds himself. The conscious personality has entirely vanished; will and discernment are lost. All feelings and thoughts are being in the direction determined by the

hypnotizer. Under the influence of a suggestion, he
will undertake the accomplishment of certain acts
with irresistible impetuosity. This impetuosity is
the more irresistible in the case of crowds, from the
fact that, the suggestion being the same for all the
individuals of the crowd, it gains in strength by
reciprocity. Moreover, by the mere fact that he
forms part of an organized crowd, a man descends
several rungs in the ladder of civilization. Isolated,
he may be a cultured individual; in a crowd, he is a
barbarian—that is, a creature acting by instinct. He
possesses the spontaneity, the violence, the
ferocity, and also the enthusiasm and heroism of
primitive beings, whom he further tends to
resemble by the facility with which he allows
himself to be induced to commit acts contrary to his
most obvious interests and his best known habits.
An individual in a crowd is a grain of, and amid
other grains of, sand, which the wind stirs up at
will."

Professor Frederick Morgan Davenport, in his *Primitive Traits in
Religious Revivals*, says:

"The mind of the crowd is strangely like that of a
primitive man. Most of the people in it may be far
from primitive in emotion, in thought, in
character; nevertheless, the result tends always to
be the same. Stimulation immediately begets
action. Reason is in abeyance. The cool, rational
speaker has little chance beside the skillful
emotional orator. The crowd thinks in images, and
speech must take this form to be accessible to it.
The images are not connected, by any natural bond,
and they take each other's place like the slides of a

magic lantern. It follows from this, of course, that appeals to the imagination have paramount influence.

"The crowd is united and governed by emotion rather than by reason. Emotion is the natural bond, for men differ much less in this respect than in intellect. It is also true that in a crowd of a thousand men, the amount of emotion actually generated and existing is far greater than the sum which might conceivably be obtained by adding together the emotions of the individuals taken by themselves. The explanation of this is that the attention of the crowd is always directed either by the circumstances of the occasion or by the speaker to certain common ideas—as 'salvation' in religious gatherings; and every individual in the gathering is stirred with emotion, not only because the idea or the shibboleth stirs him, but also because he is conscious that every other individual in the gathering believes in the idea or the shibboleth, and is stirred by it, too. And this enormously increases the volume of his own emotion and, consequently, the total volume of emotion in the crowd. As in the case of the primitive mind, imagination has unlocked the floodgates of emotion, which on occasion may become wild enthusiasm or demoniac frenzy."

The student of suggestion will see that not only are the emotional members of a revival audience subject to the effect of the "composite-mindedness" arising from the "psychology of the crowd" and are, thereby, weakened in the resistive power, but that they are also brought under the influence of two other very potent forms of mental suggestion. Added to the powerful suggestion of authority exercised by the revivalist, which is exerted to its fullest along lines very similar to that of the professional hypnotist, is the suggestion of imitation exerted upon each individual by the combined force of the balance of the crowd.

As Émile Durkheim observed in his psychological investigations, the average individual is "intimidated by the mass" of the crowd around him, or before him, and experiences that peculiar psychological influence exerted by the mere number of people as against his individual self. Not only does the suggestible person find it easy to respond to the authoritative suggestions of the preacher and the exhortations of his helpers, but he is also brought under the direct fire of the imitative suggestions of those on all sides who are experiencing emotional activities and who are manifesting them outwardly. Not only does the voice of the shepherd urge forward, but the tinkle of the bellwether's bell is also heard, and the imitative tendency of the flock, which causes one sheep to jump because one ahead of him does so (and so on until the last sheep has jumped), needs but the force of the example of a leader to start into motion the entire flock. This is not an exaggeration—human beings, in times of panic, fright, or deep emotion of any kind, manifest the imitative tendency of the sheep, and the tendency of cattle and horses to "stampede" under imitation.

To the student experienced in the experimental work of the psychological laboratory, there is the very closest analogy observed in the respective phenomena of the revival and hypnotic suggestion. In both cases, the attention and interest are attracted by the unusual procedure; the element of mystery and awe is induced by words and actions calculated to inspire them; the senses are tired by monotonous talk in an impressive and authoritative tone; and finally, the suggestions are projected in a commanding, suggestive manner familiar to all students of hypnotic suggestion. The subjects in both cases are prepared for the final suggestions and commands, by previously given minor suggestions, such as "stand up" or "look this way," etc., in the case of the hypnotist, and by "All those who think so-and-so, stand up" and "All who are willing to become better, stand up," etc., in the case of the revivalist. The impressionable subjects are thus accustomed to obedience to suggestion by easy stages. And finally, the commanding suggestion, "Come right up— right up—this way—right up—come, I say, come, come, COME!" etc., which takes the impressed ones right off their feet and rushes them to the front, are almost precisely the same in the hypnotic experiment or séance, on the one hand, and the sensational revival on the other. Every good revivalist would make a good hypnotic operator, and every good hypnotic operator would make a good revivalist if his mind was turned in that direction.

In the revival, the person giving the suggestions has the advantage of breaking down the resistance of his audience by arousing their sentiments and emotions. Tales depicting the influence of mother, home, and heaven; songs telling, "Yes, mother, I'll be there"; and personal appeals to the revered associations of one's past and early life tend to reduce one to the state of emotional response, and render them most susceptible to strong, repeated suggestions along the same line. Young people and hysterical women are especially susceptible to this form of emotional suggestion. Their feelings are stirred, and the will is influenced, by the preaching, the songs, and the personal appeals of the co-workers of the revivalist.

The most sacred sentimental memories are reawakened for the moment, and old conditions of mind are reinduced. "Where Is My Wandering Boy Tonight?" brings forth tears to many a one to whom the memory of the mother is sacred, and the preaching that the mother is dwelling in a state of bliss beyond the skies, from which the unconverted child is cut off unless he professes faith, serves to move many to action for the time being. The element of fear is also invoked in the revival—not so much as formerly, it is true, but still to a considerable extent and more subtly. The fear of a sudden death in an unconverted condition is held over the audience, and "Why not now—why not tonight?" is asked him, accompanied by the hymn, "Oh, Why Do You Wait, Dear Brother?" As Davenport says:

"It is well known that the employment of symbolic
images immensely increases the emotion of an
audience. The vocabulary of revivals abounds in
them—the cross, the crown, the angel band, hell,
heaven. Now vivid imagination and strong feeling
and belief are states of mind favorable to suggestion
as well as to impulsive action. It is also true that the
influence of a crowd, largely in sympathy with the
ideas suggested, is thoroughly coercive or
intimidating upon the individual sinner. There is
considerable professed conversion which results
in the beginning from little more than this form of
social pressure, and which may never develop
beyond it. Finally, the inhibition of all extraneous
ideas is encouraged in revival assemblies both by
prayer and by speech. There is, therefore, extreme
sensitiveness to suggestion. When to these
conditions of negative consciousness on the part of
an audience there has been added a conductor of
the meetings who has a high hypnotic potential,
such as John Wesley or Charles Grandison Finney,
or who is only a thoroughly persuasive and
magnetic personality, such as George Whitefield,
there may easily be an influence exerted upon
certain individuals of a crowd which closely
approaches the abnormal or thoroughly hypnotic.
When this point is not reached, there is still a great
amount of highly acute, though normal,
suggestibility to be reckoned with."

The persons who show signs of being influenced are then "labored
with" by either the revivalist or his co-workers. They are urged to
surrender their will and "leave it all to the Lord." They are told to
"Give yourself to God, now, right now, this minute" or to "Only

believe now, and you shall be saved" or "Won't you give yourself to Jesus?" etc. They are exhorted and prayed with; arms are placed around their shoulders, and every art of emotional, persuasive suggestion is used to make the sinner "give up."

Edwin Diller Starbuck in his *The Psychology of Religion* relates a number of instances of the experiences of converted persons at revivals. One person wrote as follows:

> **"My will seemed wholly at the mercy of others, particularly of the revivalist. There was absolutely no intellectual element. It was pure feeling. There followed a period of ecstasy. I was bent on doing good and was eloquent in appealing to others. The state of moral exaltation did not continue. It was followed by a complete relapse from orthodox religion."**

Davenport has the following to say in reply to the claim that the old methods of influencing converts at a revival have passed away with the crude theology of the past:

> **"I lay particular stress upon this matter here because, while the employment of irrational fear in revivals has largely passed away, the employment of the hypnotic method has not passed away. There has rather been a recrudescence and a conscious strengthening of it because the old prop of terror is gone. And it cannot be too vigorously emphasized that such a force is not a 'spiritual' force in any high and clear sense at all, but is rather uncanny and psychic and obscure. And the method itself needs to be greatly refined before it can ever be of any spiritual benefit whatever. It is thoroughly primitive and belongs with the animal and instinctive means of fascination. In this bald, crude**

**form, the feline employs it upon the helpless bird
and the Indian medicine-man upon the ghost dance
votary. When used, as it has often been, upon little
children who are naturally highly suggestible, it
has no justification whatever and is mentally and
morally injurious in the highest degree. I do not see
how violent emotional throes and the use of
suggestion in its crude forms can be made
serviceable, even in the cases of hardened sinners,
and certainly with large classes of the population
the employment of this means is nothing but
psychological malpractice. We guard with
intelligent care against quackery in physiological
obstetrics. It would be well if a sterner training and
prohibition hedged about the spiritual obstetrician,
whose function it is to guide the far more delicate
process of the new birth."**

Some who favor the methods of the revival, but who also
recognize the fact that mental suggestion plays a most important
part in the phenomena thereof, hold that the objections similar to
those advanced in this article are not valid against the methods of the
revival, inasmuch as mental suggestion, as is well known, may be used
for good purposes as well as bad—for the benefit and uplifting of
people as well as in the opposite direction. This being admitted, these
good folks argue that mental suggestion in the revival is a legitimate
method or "weapon of attack upon the stronghold of the devil." But
this argument is found to be defective when examined in its effects
and consequences. In the first place, it would seem to identify the
emotional, neurotic, and hysterical mental states induced by revival
methods with the spiritual uplift and moral regeneration which is the
accompaniment of true religious experience. It seeks to place the
counterfeit on a par with the genuine—the baleful glare of the rays of
the psychic moon with the invigorating and animating rays of the

spiritual sun. It seeks to raise the hypnotic phase to that of the "spiritual-mindedness" of man. To those who are familiar with the two classes of phenomena, there is a difference as wide as that between the poles existing between them.

As a straw showing how the wind of the best modern religious thought is blowing, we submit the following, from the recent volume entitled *Religion and Miracle*, from the pen of Rev. Dr. George A. Gordon, pastor of the New Old South Church of Boston:

> **"For this end professional revivalism, what its organizations, its staff of reports who make the figures suit the hopes of good men, the system of advertisements, and the exclusion or suppression of all sound critical comment, the appeals to emotion and the use of means which have no visible connection with grace and cannot by any possibility lead to glory, is utterly inadequate. The world waits for the vision, the passion, the simplicity, and the stern truthfulness of the Hebrew prophet; it awaits the imperial breadth and moral energy of the Christian apostle to the nations; it awaits the teacher who, like Christ, shall carry his doctrine in a great mind and a great character."**

While there have undoubtedly been many instances of persons attracted originally by the emotional excitement of the revival, and afterward leading worthy, religious lives in accordance with the higher spiritual nature, still in too many cases the revival has exerted but a temporary effect for good upon the persons yielding to the excitement and, after the stress has passed, has resulted in creating an indifference and even an aversion for true religious feeling. The reaction is often equal to the original action. The consequences of "backsliding" are well known in all churches, after the spirited revival. In others, there is merely awakened a susceptibility to emotional excitement, which causes the individual to undergo repeated stages of "conversion" at each revival, and a subsequent "backsliding" after the influence of the meeting is withdrawn.

Moreover, it is a fact known to psychologists that persons who have given way to the emotional excitement and excesses of the typical revival are rendered afterward far more suggestible and open to "isms," fads, and false religions than before. The people flocking to the support of the various pseudo-religious adventurers and impostors of the age are generally found to be the same people who were previously the most ardent and excitable converts of the revival. The ranks of the "Messiahs," "Elijahs," and "Prophets of the Dawn," who have appeared in great numbers in this country and England during the past fifty years, have been recruited almost exclusively from those who have previously "experienced" the revival fervor in the orthodox churches. It is the old story of the training of the hypnotic subject. Especially harmful is this form of emotional intoxication among young people and women.

It must be remembered that the period of adolescence is one in which the mental nature of the individual is undergoing great changes. It is a period noted for peculiar development of the emotional nature, the sex nature, and the religious nature. The existing conditions at this period render the psychic debauchery of the revival, séance, or hypnotic exhibition particularly harmful. Excessive emotional excitement, coupled with mystery, fear, and awe, at this period of life, often results in morbid and abnormal conditions arising in after life. As Davenport well says: "It is no time for the shock of fear or the agony of remorse. The only result of such misguided religious zeal is likely to be a strengthening in many cases of those tendencies, especially in females, toward morbidity and hysteria, toward darkness and doubt."

There are other facts connected with the close relation existing between abnormal religious excitement and the undue arousing of the sexual nature, which are well known to all students of the subject, but which cannot be spoken of here. As a hint, however, the following from Davenport will serve its purpose:

"At the age of puberty, there is an organic process at
work which pushes into activity at nearly the same
time the sexual and the spiritual. There is no proof,
however, of the causation of the latter by the
former. But it does appear to be true that the two are
closely associated at the point in the physical
process where they branch in different directions,
that at that critical period, any radical excitation of
the one has its influence upon the other. A careful
consideration of this important statement will
serve to explain many things that have sorely
perplexed many good people in the past, in
connection with revival excitement in a town,
camp meetings, etc. This apparent influence of the
devil, which so worried our forefathers, is seen to
be but the operation of natural psychological and
physiological laws. To understand it is to have the
remedy at hand."

But what do the authorities say of the revival of the future—the
new revival—the real revival? Let Professor Davenport speak for the
critics—he is well adapted for the task. He says:

"There will be, I believe, far less use of the revival
meeting as a crass coercive instrument for
overriding the will and overwhelming the reason of
the individual man. The influence of public
religious gatherings will be more indirect, more
unobtrusive. It will be recognized that
hypnotization and forced choices weaken the soul,
and there will be no attempt to press to decision in
so great a matter under the spell of excitement and
contagion and suggestion. The converts may be
few. They may be many. They will be measured not
by the capacity of the preacher for administrative

hypnotism, but rather by the capacity for unselfish friendship of every Christian man and woman. But of this I think we may be confident—the days of religious effervescence and passional unrestraint are dying. The days of intelligent, undemonstrative, and self-sacrificing piety are dawning. To do justly, to love mercy, to walk humbly with God—these remain cardinal tests of the divine in man.

"Religious experience is an evolution. We go on from the rudimentary and the primitive to the rational and the spiritual. And, believe Paul, the mature fruit of the spirit is not the subliminal up rush, the lapse of inhibition, but rational love, joy, peace, long-suffering, kindness, goodness, faithfulness, meekness—self-control."

11

The Law of
Compensation

*T*he purpose of this editorial, as well as the purpose back of this magazine itself, is to help men and women weave the "shoddy" threads of their experiences, hardships, failures, and struggles into a rich garment of truth and understanding that will clothe their efforts, finally, with success and happiness, to help people learn to draw a winning hand out of the discard of life's failures and experiences.—Editor.

The death of a dear friend, wife, brother, lover, which seemed nothing but privation, somewhat later assumes the aspect of a guide or genius, for it commonly operates revolutions in our way of life, terminates an epoch of infancy or of youth which was waiting to be closed, breaks up a wonted occupation or a household, or style of living, and allows the formation of new ones more friendly to the growth of character!

—EMERSON

The law of compensation is no respecter of persons. It operates for or against the rich and the poor alike. It is as immutable as the law of gravitation. If it were not so, this planet which we call earth would not roll on and on throughout immeasurable time and space, keeping ever in its true course. It is the equalizing force which balances the "eternal scales" and keeps the planets in their places.

The law of compensation permits no voids or hollow places anywhere in the universe. What is taken away from one place is replaced by something else.

Read Emerson's essay on compensation. It will lay the foundation in your mind for the development of that much-sought quality called "balance" or "sense of proportions" which marks the man or the woman who attains to great heights in the field of business, industry, or the professions.

The law of compensation never seems pushed for time, often deferring both its penalties and rewards over long periods. That which it exacts from one, generally as a penalty, is given over to the next generation as a reward. That which it takes away from the individual, it gives back to the offspring, or to the race as a whole. The law of compensation is no cheater, nor will it tolerate cheating. It squares its accounts to the penny and to every act and thought, demanding its debts and paying its rewards with an unvarying exactness.

> Love, beauty, joy, and worship are forever building, unbuilding, and rebuilding in each man's soul.

Crime and punishment grow out of one stem.

The world war was a tremendous shock to humanity and a tremendous loss to the world, but already we can begin to see the compensating advantages that grew out of it.

For example, we have learned the folly of trying to "impose" rulership from the top without the consent of those ruled, through so-called "divine" righters. We have been reminded of Lincoln's famous words concerning a "government of the people, by the people, for the people," and we know that his idea was sound.

We have learned, also, the folly of religious and racial intolerance; that all the people, of whatever religious belief or race, can fight for one common cause. We learned this because we saw Catholics and Protestants, Jews and Gentiles, fighting side by side in the trenches, never stopping to question one another as to race or creed. Somehow, we cannot get away from believing that this same spirit of tolerance will prevail among these people in their everyday relationships, because they learned during the war not only that this was possible, but that it actually was the sensible thing for all.

As another example, we commended to learn, with the close of the world war, that a part of the purpose of life is to be decent to one another here on earth, thereby reaping a part of our reward for virtue now, instead of waiting for it to come to us in the hereafter, in a world that we know not of. Out of this feeling is bound to come tolerance such as the world has never known before.

What finer thought could come to the human race? What sounder philosophy than the belief that a part of one's reward for virtue may be reaped here and now, by recognizing the law of compensation and governing one's self accordingly.

The law of compensation both rewards and punishes! The punishment, as well as the reward, takes on every possible guise. Sometimes it seems self-inflicted, while at other times it seems to come from causes beyond the individual control, but come it will, in one guise or another. There is one means of approach which no human being can cut off, and that is through the conscience. Punishment is often visited upon a man through his conscience (or imagination) when it exists nowhere else. As evidence of this— evidence that might be multiplied by a million similar cases—read the following account of a bank clerk who stole some money and fled, with the "law"—the unrelenting law of compensation—on his trail for eighteen years, and watch the workings of this law as you read.

At the end of eighteen years, he found himself again in the United States. He was getting old. The vital force in him was flagging; the courage that had driven him through his trials and adventures assumed a new turn. It drove him back to the scene of his theft. He could go no further but in one direction. His bark turned homeward.

One morning, the wanderer walked in upon the sheriff of his home town and said simply, "I'm Bill Jones."

"Pleased to meet you, Mr. Jones," said the officer, without taking his feet off his desk.

The haunted man was struck dumb.

"What can I do for you?" asked the sheriff, smiling wryly.

"You don't understand," said Jones. "I'm the fellow you've been hunting so long."

"Not me, my friend," said the officer, sensing a lunatic.

"No, maybe not. It's been so long ago," pondered the returned man, rubbing his eyes. "I'm the man who stole the three thousand dollars from the Merchants Loan Bank."

"Well, what of it?" the sheriff wanted to know. "There hasn't been any such bank for ten years."

The rover wavered and asked if he might sit down. He pondered a long time while the officer watched him uneasily. He looked like a man who was struggling with some desperate problem, trying to plumb some deep and terrible mystery.

❧

Self-Inflicted Punishment

"Do you keep a file of men that are wanted?" he asked the sheriff.
"Yep."

"I wonder if you would do me a favor?"

"Sure."

"Would you look up the files of July, eighteen years ago, and see if a man named Bill Jones was wanted for stealing from the Merchants Loan?"

The sheriff went through his books. There was no record of such a case. A little inquiry developed that the bank had never let out a whisper of the defalcation. The officers had preferred pocketing the loss to risking a run. And so Bill Jones had fled round the world, hunted for eighteen years by a phantom, when he might have lived securely in the next county and never been sought or taken.

"I punished myself all those years," the aging man murmured bitterly. "I suffered every torture a man can know—for nothing."

"I punished myself all those years!"

Ah, there is the thought to which you can profitably direct sober reflection! "I punished myself."

In each human heart lies the power to visit upon the person, from within, joy or sorrow, according to the extent to which one's efforts are made to conform to the law of compensation or permitted to run counter against it.

Only truth can permanently prevail. All else must pass on.

There never was any man-made law placed on the statute books, and there never will be any such law placed there, which cannot be broken and the consequences avoided now and then, by shrewd and cunning men, but no man has yet been smart enough to thwart the workings of the law of compensation. That law is man-proof. The more man tinkers with it, the less chance he stands of escaping its consequences, unless he earnestly studies it with the object of conforming to its principles!

By turning back the pages of history, we learn that most of the great men of the past—those whose names have lived beyond the grave—were men who suffered much, who sacrificed, who met with failure and defeat, yet went smiling on to the end of this physical existence without bitterness in their hearts.

The pages of history are full of such men, from Socrates and the man from Galilee on down to the present, but a case that particularly claims our attention just now, on account of the fact that the principal still lives, is that of Knut Hamsun, whose story is briefly told in the following press dispatch:

❧

A Tramp Wins the Nobel Prize for Literature

The Nobel Prize in literature has been awarded, nearly fifty thousand dollars, to Knut Hamsun, whom probably not one American in one hundred ever heard of.

But Hamsun was for years a streetcar conductor in Chicago and a longshoreman in New York City. He has been a dishwasher in a restaurant, a coal passer on a tramp steamer, a house painter, a writer of scientific essays, a porter in a hotel, a deck hand, and many others things.

Like O. Henry, he was for years a forlorn, friendless, and homeless person, wandering over the face of the earth, often without money or food, a sleeper on park benches.

Now he receives the most glittering single prize offered anywhere in the world to literary genius, awarded by a committee of experts.

Hamsun was discharged as a trolley car conductor because "he never could remember the names of streets." The Chicago superintendent said he seemed too stupid even for skipper for a Halsted streetcar. So he went to New York, worked on the docks several months, and then shipped as a seaman on a fishing smack for Newfoundland. Wherever he went, he was always scribbling on paper.

Finally, he published his *Pan*, a lyrical novel of epic power. The volume has been translated into seventeen languages, of which English was one of the last.

His two most notable novels are *Shallow Soil* and *Hunger*. The last has neither plot, beginning, nor end. Nor is the name or age of the hero given. It describes what happens to a man who cannot get work in a great city, either as a writer or a laborer, and is forced to go hungry after pawning most of his clothes. The novel leaves the man exactly where it found him—friendless, homeless, nameless. No one who reads it will ever forget it.

This was Knut Hamsun's own experience.

Now, at sixty, he has worldwide fame, a fifty-thousand-dollar prize, and a handsome country estate in Norway, and his gates will henceforth be besieged by publishers.

As Mark Twain says, the only difference between truth and fiction is that fiction has to stick to what seems possible. Truth doesn't.

> Men and women are beginning to learn that they need not wait
> for a world that they know not of, beyond the grim shadow
> called death, to find happiness.

Verily, we repeat, out of hardship and failure comes strength! This
seems like unsound philosophy while we are experiencing the
"hardship and failure," but all who survive these cleansing experiences know differently.

My own will eventually come to me, and I will recognize it when it
arrives if I keep always in mind the fact that the law of compensation
is eternally at work, because if I do this, I will know that "my own"
will harmonize with and correspond to my conduct in life toward my
fellowmen.

Ten years of observation have taught me much concerning the
workings of this law of compensation. I have seen it place men on the
highest pinnacle of what the world calls "success," and I have seen it
topple them over and roll them right back to the bottom from which
they started.

Twelve years ago, I enjoyed the acquaintance of a banker in
Washington, D.C. This man began as a dentist, and fortune seemed
to smile upon him. He began the business of loaning money, in small
amounts, at exorbitant rates, as a side issue. He became so successful
at this that he finally organized a bank and was elected as its president.
This gave him greater prestige and additional financial power; so he
began to reach out and buy up real estate, taking a heavy toll from
every transaction. The people began to complain of his usurious rates
of interest and his tightfisted business methods, but from all outside
appearances, he continued to gather power and prosper.

I was a client of this man's bank. When I needed money, he loaned
it to me, but his rates of interest to me were always moderate and in
keeping with the rates charged at other banks. I often wondered why
he was so fair and liberal with me while he was so unfair and exacting
with others. I owned a prosperous school of mechanical engineering.

I learned, by and by, why this banker was so liberal with me. He wanted that school, and he finally got it. When he had loaned money to me so that he knew I was over my head in the case of an emergency, he closed me out.

That transaction was a blow to me; yet, in the light of subsequent years' experience, I know that it was a blessing in disguise, probably one of the greatest that ever came my way, because it forced me out of a business which played no part in developing strong moral fiber, or laying the foundation for a worldwide service to my fellowmen such as I am rendering today.

I could not prove that this temporary failure was a deliberate part of a great plan to direct my efforts into more constructive channels, but if some power had been putting such a plan into operation, it could not have been more successfully conducted than it was. That which was taken away from me ten years ago has been more than repaid within the last three or four years. The law of compensation has squared accounts with me, and still the reward seems to be coming my way.

But, there was another and different reason for telling of this banker. Two years ago, I went back to Washington for a short visit. It is natural for a person to want to go back to those old stomping grounds where, in bygone days, he experienced either great joy or great sorrow. When I got to Washington, I strolled down Fourteenth Street, thinking to look the banker over and supposing, of course, that I would find a few stories added to his bank building and a prosperous, strong bank, such as I had known his to be ten years ago.

When I got to the bank building, I found that the banking fixtures had been removed, the bank had gone out of business, and the splendid banking house had been turned into a lunch room!

I went on down Fourteenth Street to the $75,000 mansion which this banker owned ten years ago, but it was occupied now by new tenants and no longer belonged to him.

Inquiry proved that this erstwhile successful banker had been reduced almost overnight to the ranks from which he had ascended, for reasons which seemed not very clear to anyone!

He was down and out!

The silent, heavy hand had descended upon his head, and he had gone down in spite of every resource at his command. Back of that heavy hand was a force that was augmented by every disgruntled depositor whom this man had come in contact with in his bank, every widow who had felt his "own hand" under a mortgage foreclosure, every property owner who had been "squeezed" preparatory to the purchase, by this bank, of his land.

Emerson has so well said:

> **"Every excess causes a defect, every defect an excess. Every sweet hath its sour, every evil its good. Every faculty which is a receiver of pleasure has an equal penalty put on its abuse. For every grain of wit, there is a grain of folly. For everything you have missed, you have gained something else; and for everything you gain, you lose something. If riches increase, they are increased that use them. If the gatherer gathers too much, nature takes out of the man what she puts into his treasure chest, swells the estate, but kills the owner. Nature hates monopolies and exceptions. The waves of the sea do not more speedily seek a level from their loftiest tossing, than the varieties of condition tend to equalize themselves. There is always bearing, the strong, the rich, the fortunate, substantially on the same ground with all others!"**

What greater work is there than that of helping people weave the shoddy threads of failures, mistakes, and heartaches into a beautiful garment that will clothe their efforts in a final success.

When my former associate lost sight of the high ideals, the humanitarian aims and purposes which actuated me in editing *Hill's Golden Rule Magazine*, and was no longer able to hold principle above the dollar, was no longer actuated by the spirit to serve instead of the desire to get, his change of attitude forced me to disconnect myself from him. In doing so, it practically meant that two years of labor was lost; it means that new contacts must be formed, that new subscribers must be secured, that my work must all be done over again. Yet, only three short months have elapsed since I decided to take the step which told all the world that I stood for principle above the dollar, for humanity above the individual, and I have been more than compensated for taking this stand by the sweeping storm of protest that swept down on my former publisher from those who sensed what had happened, and the corresponding pledge of support of this magazine which has come to me from those same people.

In the light of every experience which I have cataloged, and in the light of every observation which I have made with relation to others, I am bound to say frankly and boldly that where principle stands in the way of pecuniary gain, there is only one thing to do and that is to support principle; where the cause of the individual is in conflict with the cause of humanity as a whole, support the cause of humanity! All who would thus boldly assert themselves must sacrifice, temporarily, but just as sure as the sun rises in the east and sets in the west, their just reward will come to them further along the line, when the law of compensation begins to get down to business.

One of the very best ways to teach a child that a hot coffee pot will burn is to explain, in minute detail, that hot surfaces always burn, then turn your back and let the child do a little experimenting with its fingers. One lesson will be about right. Some of us "children grown tall" learn in the same way.

12

The Golden Rule
as a Passkey to
All Achievement

*T*his article took form in the editor's mind while he was listening to an intensely practical scientist, and it so crowded his attention that it gave him no rest until he had placed it on paper. It may bring you the passkey to achievement and understanding which you have been seeking all your life.

A very learned man entertained me at lunch yesterday. For more than two hours, I listened to his philosophy of life.

This man is a scientist of international reputation.

He made two statements, however, which were in direct conflict with each other. First, he said there was no panacea for the present ills of the world.

Then, he told me the story of the structure of the human body, of its interesting growth from a single tiny cell. He traced the history of the cells which compose the human body and showed me how millions upon millions of these tiny little creatures cooperate in the business of keeping the body alive and healthy, in compliance with an unvarying law.

It was an interesting story. This learned scientist made it so with his graphic illustrations and comparisons. In his climax, he made a statement which caused this article to begin to shape itself in my mind. He said that the human body would never die if it were not for the fact that some of the body cells quit their practice of cooperating with the other cells. He said that as long as there is complete harmony among the various groups of cells which constitute the human body, as long as each group carries on the work which it is supposed to carry on, perfect health will exist in the entire human body.

All the while, I was trying to harmonize his statement that there was no panacea for the present world's ills with his statement that the human body would live forever if all the tiny little cells which constitute the body continued to cooperate in harmony.

Before my mind's eye, I could see an underlying principle which affects not alone the various groups of cells in the human body, but which affects the entire human race. This man of science had unconsciously started my mind to work along lines entirely new to it, and before I left him, I had drawn this conclusion, a conclusion which I pass on to you with the feeling that the simple analogy which I have drawn may enable you to see that which I saw as I listened to my host talk of a principle which is as immutable as the law of gravitation itself: namely, that there is a panacea for the world's ills, and that this panacea is nothing more nor less than the principle which insures perfect health in the human body, as long as the cells which constitute the body are working harmoniously, and insures death when a portion of these cells cease to cooperate and function normally.

I hope I am not dealing in terms too abstract to carry my exact meaning. To make myself more clearly understood, I will draw for you the same comparison which I drew for myself while this man was talking.

I saw, in my imagination, the entire human race, every living human being on earth, all gathered in one spot and standing in such a position as to form the perfect outline of a human being. At a distance, this seething mass of humanity would resemble one enormous human being. I could see health and success and prosperity for the whole mass as long as there was no discord or misunderstanding between the individuals who constituted the whole. I could see some of the human beings plowing the ground while others were sowing seed and getting ready to produce food. I could see some of the individuals of that enormous gathering working on clothing. I would see still others entertaining the mass with music and causing each individual to be happy and contented.

Perfect harmony prevailed in this imaginary picture.

Every individual had plenty to eat and plenty to wear. All were happy and contented. Sorrow and grief were not to be found.

Then, with sudden switch of the imagination, I saw the picture from another angle, an angle which is comparable to the story of the human cells of which the scientist had been telling me. Away down toward the bottom of this great mass of human beings, at a point which would correspond to one of the imaginary giant's feet, I saw two tiny little human beings get into an argument. They came to blows. Other human beings began to rush up and join in the argument. Pretty soon, one of the entire feet of the imaginary giant had discontinued its regular business, and the "human cells" of which the foot was composed were fighting among themselves. They no longer cooperated. They no longer functioned normally.

Pretty soon, the entire body began to feel the loss of one of its feet. It was crippled. It tried to walk but could not move. Other parts of the body commenced to suffer. The body, as a whole, commenced to suffer with hunger because the loss of its foot prevented it from producing food.

Slowly, that enormous body began to wither and go into decay. I could not help comparing it to the individual human body which withers, goes into decay, and finally into death when any group of cells ceases to carry on its normal work.

There is a remedy which is often applied with successful results when the individual cells of the human body begin to "lie down on the job," and that remedy is to re-establish harmony and cooperation among the cells to the end that they will again function normally.

That same remedy is the one, and probably the only one, which will save the human race and bring it back to normal, healthy, constructive living once more.

The same principle which causes the tiny human body cells to function and cooperate in peace and harmony while the individual enjoys a healthy, happy human body applies with equal precision to the entire human race.

A wise philosopher has said that we cannot indict a whole race. But, it may be too much to expect one man to be a sound philosopher and also a successful automobile manufacturer.

That which affects a single human being affects, also, to some extent, the neighborhood in which that person lives; and that which affects an entire neighborhood affects, to some extent, the entire world. That which brings sorrow and suffering and hunger in one family may not be felt, directly, in another family, but you may be sure that a change really takes place.

The late world war has taught the human race the folly of believing that one nation or group of people can suffer without their suffering affecting the entire world. We are all paying for the cost of the war, no matter which country seems to have won or lost.

Not alone are we all paying now, but we have created a debt which will burden the generations yet to come. When lack of harmony grips the human race, we all suffer just as the human body suffers when one little group of cells ceases to cooperate in harmony.

So much for these comparisons!

Now let's go back to the remedy—to the cause which will produce peace and harmony and success among the various groups of "human cells" which constitute the human family on this earth.

This remedy has been discovered. It is not a new remedy, but it is a sure one. It is nothing more nor less than the Golden Rule philosophy.

What a pity the schools of medicine and the law schools and the mechanical engineering schools and all the other schools have not given over part of their curriculum to teaching their students the necessity of carrying on their vocation under the Golden Rule principle. What a loss the human race has suffered because it has been taught to look upon the Golden Rule philosophy as a mere theory instead of viewing it as a practical, workable principle which affects favorably all who understand and apply it in business, finance, industry, and economics.

Every practicing physician and every chiropractor and every osteopath and every other healer on earth should have been taught the absolute necessity of recommending the Golden Rule, in plentiful quantities, along with his other remedies for human bodily ills.

And every lawyer should have been taught, while learning the profession of law, to settle all cases out of court under the Golden Rule principle, whenever possible. It should have been laid down as an established principle, and so taught in every law school on earth, that any lawyer failing to use his best efforts to bring his clients to see the advantage of settling their grievances under the Golden Rule principle would immediately be classed as a "quack."

And, every business college teacher on earth should have been trained to teach the boys and girls under his tutorship to apply the Golden Rule in all business relationships; that to fail to do so would bring failure and reproach from the business world.

What a regrettable fact it is that the human race still remains in comparative ignorance of the possibilities of the simple Golden Rule philosophy as a basis for all business dealings. The world has never accepted this philosophy except in theory, yet it is unquestionably the panacea for the world's ills, from the least to the greatest of the ills.

Before I began this article, I scanned the pages of my daily paper, and my eyes fell upon the following news item:

Dog under "Arrest" Acquitted When He Licks Boy's Hand

Justice Daniel Mickey of Evanston returned a verdict of acquittal in the case of Spug, a black dog of unknown pedigree, charged with grave crimes against the person of Arnold Martin, 12. He bit him.

Arnold, son of John C. Martin, 921 Tenth Street, Evanston, threw a newspaper up the porch of C. F. Hess, 1335 Gregory Avenue. When he drew his

hand back, there was something hanging on it, Spug.

The boy told his father, after standing in front of the Hess home and telling the world. Police took Spug to the station house, and a warrant was issued for Mr. Hess.

In court, Mr. Martin was angry. Mr. Hess was indignant. Arnold Martin was relenting; Spug wagged his silly tail.

Arnold Martin happened to pet Spug thoughtlessly, and the dog jumped into his lap and proceeded to lick his face and hands frantically. The boy laughed, struggling, Mr. Martin snickered, Mr. Hess let a tear trickle down his cheek, and the case was over.

"Discharged," said the court.

I hope you see in this news item that which this writer saw when he read it, because it embodies the whole of the Golden Rule principle and shows exactly how that principle works when properly applied.

That little dumb animal which we call a dog, either consciously or unconsciously, tapped the power which rules this universe, keeps the stars in their places, determines the destiny of men on this earth, and controls every atom of matter throughout the universe.

Read the foregoing paragraph again, because it carries a broad statement which, if true, will give you the clue that will help you solve your own problems and help you serve the human race to advantage.

The little dog saved its own life—saved it by applying the principle which underlies the Golden Rule. How long, oh, God! how long until we little children of the human race will learn to apply this Golden Rule principle with as much intelligence as this little dog applied it? How long must we go on suffering and destroying one another and helping to cut down the human race through envy and hatred and jealousy and greed? How long must we go on suffering and passing the cause for our suffering on to our offspring before we will awake to the realization that the simple injunction laid down in the Golden Rule will bring us peace and happiness on this earth?

> Jews and Gentiles, Catholics and Protestants, brothers all—and we see no reason for inciting them to strife because of race or religion.

There has never been a war, not a labor trouble, nor a misunderstanding between two human beings which could not have been averted through proper understanding and application of the Golden Rule philosophy.

Most of us are interested in getting some other member or members of the race to do that which we want them to do. We lie awake nights trying to think out schemes whereby we can get another person to do that which we want him to do. We know exactly how we could make a million dollars, or build a great business, or reduce the cost of living, or render mankind some other great service if—and that eternal if is this:

"If" we could get people to do that which we want them to do!

Seemingly, it has never occurred to most of us that there is an infallible method through which we can get other people to do that which we want them to do. Seemingly, it has never occurred to us that we can get other people to act toward us as we wish them to by simply acting that way toward them first and keeping it up until they respond!

Do you get the full significance of that which you have just read?

If you do, you are to be congratulated, because you will never again complain that anyone failed to do that which you wanted him to do. You will know how to get that which you want by first giving the same thing to some other member or group of members of the human race.

Furthermore, you will never again be guilty of putting into motion a cause which will bring suffering and sorrow and hunger and deprivation to any member of the human race, because you will know beforehand that this same result will eventually come back to curse you.

If you get the full significance of the foregoing, you will never again place another person in any situation wherein you, yourself, would not be delighted to take his place and let him take yours.

If you understand and believe in the principle just outlined, which is nothing more nor less than the Golden Rule philosophy as it applies in the practical, everyday life, you will never permit one of your own children to grow into maturity without thoroughly understanding and learning the advantages of applying this principle.

This message, I fully realize, is not for the entire human race; it is only for those rare souls who have evolved to that state of understanding in which they can check up, in their own experiences, and draw comparisons which will prove all that I have stated. It is mainly for those who tried and failed, and tried and failed again and again, until they are now ready to stop and ask themselves the reason why they have failed.

You can test yourself, before laying aside this magazine, as to how much evolution has done for you. If you are contented to pass this thought by without resolving, with that grim determination that knows no defeat, to put this Golden Rule philosophy to work as a part of your own philosophy, you must suffer and fail and undergo some more grief and reverses, because you are not one of those rare human beings who has learned that there is a cause for every effect!

There is still another thought I would like to leave with you, and it is this:

We learn more about a principle the moment we try to teach it to someone else; therefore, do not rest contented with your own understanding of this Golden Rule principle. Go out into the highways and the byways of life, into the shops and factories, and begin to explain it to others. The more you try to explain it, the more you will find out about it yourself, until finally you will attain that rare degree of mastership which will enable you to see that the salvation of the human race from ultimate destruction depends upon the race learning the power back of the Golden Rule and applying that power for the preservation of the race.

Who can profit most through the universal application of the Golden Rule? Just how can any individual profit by applying the Golden Rule in all relationships with other people?

These are pertinent questions that we ought to ask ourselves, and we should never cease searching for the answer. The man who earns his living by day's wages, and who finds it hard to produce enough with his hands to feed and clothe his body, finds it hard to accept the Golden Rule philosophy as applying to him. On every hand, he sees what looks to him like injustice and conspiracy against him. He believes that he receives too little for the amount of work he performs. All around him, he sees others living in better circumstances. Fate seems to have dealt him an unfair blow.

Now, please follow me with close thought because here is the point at which millions of people are making a fundamental mistake that cuts them off from that rich heritage of happiness and success which could be theirs if they understood and applied a simple fundamental principle, and that principle is the Golden Rule.

These people who see the injustice of life which has sentenced them to toil and strife and unhappiness and grief and poverty feel very keenly the sting of this injustice, or that which they believe to be injustice. Feeling as they do, they reflect their feelings in their faces, in every movement of their bodies, and in every act toward their fellowmen! Unconsciously, they so conduct themselves that they impress others about them as possessing an "ingrown" disposition which is inhibitory and repelling to others. As a result of this impression, they have no real intimate friends or associates. No one takes the trouble to throw opportunity their way. Others keep away from them as far as possible. While they are inwardly condemning their employers or the public whom they are supposed to serve and please, the employers or the public are searching for ways and means of dispensing with their services on account of their disagreeable attitude toward life.

Remember this: There are only two kinds of forces in this universe. One attracts, and the other repels! You are a force, and you belong in one or the other of these classifications. You either attract people or repel them. And, remember this also, that all whom you attract are in harmony with your own attitude toward life. That is why you attract them. Like attracts like. Men of wealth and success are attracted to one another. Professional tramps and down-and-outers are attracted to one another. This principle applies to every atom, molecule, and electron throughout this universe.

To seek a day's pay for half a day's work is not observing the Golden Rule. To think of yourself and yours and forget your duty to your neighborhood, your fellow workers, or your associates is not observing the Golden Rule. To permit another person to render you service for which you do not give adequate pay is not observing the Golden Rule.

Check up on yourself and see if you are making any of these fundamental mistakes, and if you are, you will begin to find the reason for your unhappy, poverty-stricken condition in life. That is, you will discover the reason for your "unlucky" lot in life unless you are one of those peculiar human beings who absolutely refuse to face any condition that shows him his real self.

You can change the attitude of others toward you by first changing your attitude toward others!

Please read the foregoing sentence again. It is worth it.

This writer must make a confession before closing, and it is this: He knows this principle will work because he has tried it. You never will know whether it will work or not until you try it. This lesson might as well never have been written, as far as you are concerned, unless you experiment with the fundamental principle with which it deals. There might as well be no such law as that embodied in the Golden Rule, as far as you are concerned, unless you apply it in your relationships with your fellow sojourners here on earth.

Never mind what others are doing, or whether they are applying the Golden Rule or not. Never mind the injustices and wrongs of the world. Never mind those who fail to apply the Golden Rule in their dealings with you. Your job is to master yourself and direct your efforts in the direction that you wish them to go. If others choose to go on violating the Golden Rule, that is their misfortune, but it will not excuse you if you do the same.

This is a thought which I would like to drive home in the minds of organized labor, not as a reprimand to the workers of the world, but as a constructive, helpful suggestion that may show them the pathway to ultimate solution of their problem. I wish I had the power to clearly and definitely impress the minds of the workers of the world with the fundamental truth that they cannot succeed by committing the same error and making the same mistakes which they accuse capital of making.

To do so is not applying the Golden Rule!

No human being or group of human beings can attain success that will be permanent unless that success is built upon sound fundamentals. A temporary point of advantage may be attained through unfair means, and without observing the Golden Rule, but there is always some leveling circumstance, some evening-up process which will cut the foundation from under all whom so attain temporary advantage.

Before closing, I wish to leave this final thought with you, namely, that religion or philosophy which is merely passive is of but little value to the individual. To profit by the Golden Rule philosophy, you must do more than understand it—you must apply it. You must talk about it to others. You must teach others the advantage of applying it. To profit most by the Golden Rule, you should gain recognition in your neighborhood, place of business, or place of employment as being a person who believes in and applies the Golden Rule in all human relationships.

If you understand the power back of the Golden Rule philosophy, you can appropriate enough of that power, inside of the next twelve months, to bring you all the happiness you want. You can make this philosophy bring you wealth and material success. You can make it help you turn enemies into friends. You can make it help you attain greater success in the practice of law, medicine, engineering, or merchandising. You can make it help you earn more with a pick and shovel, if you earn your living with these implements of labor.

But, you can do none of these things unless you actually live in harmony with the Golden Rule. To merely believe in the principle is not enough. Nearly everyone believes in it, no doubt, but the trouble which the millions are making is that they are merely passive toward this principle. To profit by it, they must become active in using it. The blessings that come from applying the Golden Rule can be appropriated in no other way except through use. To believe in the Golden Rule and preach it to others carries but little, if any, weight unless you actually demonstrate it in every transaction with your fellowmen.

This writer got his first glimpse of the real possibilities back of the Golden Rule philosophy when he found it to be an expedient means of achieving an objective in life. Measure the Golden Rule by the cold standard of economics, and you will see that its use is always expedient. In dollars and cents, the Golden Rule pays handsome dividends, and this is how and why it pays:

Every person has what we call "reputation." It may be good, medium, or bad, but whatever it is, it represents the accumulated transactions which you have had with other people. One dishonest or shady transaction may make but slight difference in your life if it is followed by a long series of straightforward dealings. People come to know you by the preponderance of your tendency toward honesty or dishonesty.

When you deliberately establish a standard by which to govern yourself in all transactions with others, and that standard is the Golden Rule, you gradually build a reputation which gains you the confidence, good will, and active cooperation of all with whom you come in contact.

This is in compliance with the law of attraction, a law which you deliberately set into motion in your favor when you deal with people on the Golden Rule basis.

Reverse the principle and build your reputation out of "shady" transactions, even though no single transaction be of far-reaching importance, and by and by, the "accumulated experience" of the people who know you, which constitutes your reputation, will undermine their confidence in you and reduce you to sure failure.

There is no escape from this law.

Lastly, and perhaps of more importance than the other principles mentioned, if you understand the principle of auto-suggestion, you know the effect which every transaction has on your own mind. If you are filling your subconscious mind with the undeniable fact that you are dealing with other people always on the Golden Rule basis, you soon build such a healthy respect for yourself and develop such powerful self-confidence that nothing on earth can stop you from attaining your desires in life.

A Golden Rule consciousness, well developed in your own mind, will give you the power to attain the heights of achievement in whatever life work you may have chosen, and no one will ever care to stop you.

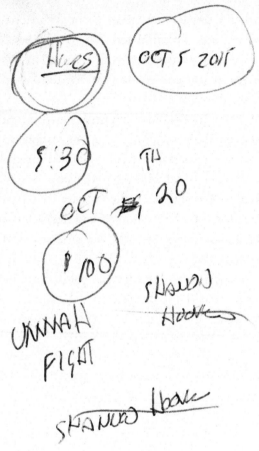

Thurs   OCT 5 2015

8:30   TH
       OCT # 20

$100
UMMAH
FIGHT

SHAWN
Hodges

SHANDO Hodge